ΠEO
PAGAN
RITES

About the Author

Isaac Bonewits is one of North America's leading experts on ancient and modern Druidism, Witchcraft, magic and the occult, and the rapidly growing Earth Religions movement. A practicing Neopagan priest, scholar, teacher, bard, and polytheologian for over thirty-five years, he has coined much of the vocabulary and articulated many of the issues that have shaped the rapidly growing Neopagan community in the United States and Canada. He is currently writing books on polytheology, dualism and its impact on modern politics, and the history of Halloween.

To Write to the Author

If you wish to contact the author or would like more information about this book, please write to the author in care of Llewellyn Worldwide and we will forward your request. Both the author and publisher appreciate hearing from you and learning of your enjoyment of this book and how it has helped you. Llewellyn Worldwide cannot guarantee that every letter written to the author can be answered, but all will be forwarded. Please write to:

Isaac Bonewits
℅ Llewellyn Worldwide
2143 Wooddale Drive, Dept. 978-0-7387-1199-7
Woodbury, Minnesota 55125-2989, U.S.A.
Please enclose a self-addressed stamped envelope for reply,
or $1.00 to cover costs. If outside U.S.A., enclose
international postal reply coupon.

Many of Llewellyn's authors have websites with
additional information and resources.
For more information, please visit our website at
http://www.llewellyn.com

ΠΕΟ
PAGAΠ
RiTES

A GUiDE TO CREATiΠG
PUBLiC RiTUALS THAT WORK

Isaac Bonewits

Llewellyn Publications
Woodbury, Minnesota

First Edition
First Printing, 2007

Book design by Donna Burch
Cover art © BrandX Pictures
Cover design by Kevin R. Brown
Editing by Connie Hill
Llewellyn is a registered trademark of Llewellyn Worldwide, Ltd.

Library of Congress Cataloging-in-Publication Data:
Bonewits, Philip Emmons Isaac.
  Neopagan rites : a guide to creating public rituals that work / Isaac Bonewits. — 1st ed.
    p.   cm.
  Includes bibliographical references (p.   ).
  ISBN: 978-0-7387-1199-7
1. Neopaganism—Rituals.   I. Title.
  BP605.N46B66   2007
  299'.94—dc22   2007032992

Originally published as *Rites of Worship* in 2003, by Dubsar House. Parts of this work have previously appeared in *The Druids' Progress* and/or *Oak Leaves* (journals of Ár nDraíocht Féin: A Druid Fellowship, Inc.), *Pentalpha Journal & Druid Chronicler, The Druid Chronicles* (Evolved).

Llewellyn Worldwide does not participate in, endorse, or have any authority or responsibility concerning private business transactions between our authors and the public.
  All mail addressed to the author is forwarded but the publisher cannot, unless specifically instructed by the author, give out an address or phone number.
  Any Internet references contained in this work are current at publication time, but the publisher cannot guarantee that a specific location will continue to be maintained. Please refer to the publisher's website for links to authors' websites and other sources.

Llewellyn Publications
A Division of Llewellyn Worldwide, Ltd.
2143 Woodedale Drive, Dept. 978-0-7387-1199-7
Woodbury, Minnesota 55125-2989, U.S.A.
www.llewellyn.com

Printed in the United States of America

Where ritual is absent, the young ones are restless or violent, there are no real elders, and the grown-ups are bewildered.

—Malidoma Patrice Somé
Ritual: Power, Healing and Community

Other Books by Isaac Bonewits

Real Magic
Authentic Thaumaturgy
The Pagan Man
Bonewits's Essential Guide to Druidism
Bonewits's Essential Guide to Witchcraft and Wicca

and
Real Energy
with Phaedra Bonewits

Dedication

This book is for my son, Arthur Shaffrey Lipp-Bonewits, with deep love for his spirit and pride in his clear-eyed assessments of adult rituals, as well as for all those others (and Others) who have taught me so much about ritual over the years.

Contents

Acknowledgments

I must acknowledge my enormous debt to Joseph Campbell, Georges Dumézil, Mircea Eliade, and James Frazer. Their pioneering work in the fields of comparative mythology and religion will not be soon forgotten. The works of Wendy Doniger O' Flaherty, Alwyn and Brinley Rees, and Anne Ross provided the seeds from which my research into Indo-European Paleopaganism has evolved, while the works of Bruce Lincoln, G. Scott Littleton, Brian Smith, and others have furthered that research considerably.

My efforts to articulate Neopagan polytheology and practice would have gotten nowhere without the writings of Margot Adler, Starhawk, and Oberon and Morning Glory Zell-Ravenheart. The works of Aleister Crowley, Janet and Stewart Farrar, Dion Fortune, Gerald Gardner, Ronald Hutton, Aidan Kelly, and Doreen Valiente were critical to my understanding of the early history of the Wiccan rituals from which most of Neopagan liturgy has grown.

The thousands of people with whom I have performed magical and religious rituals over the last thirty-five years have provided me with irreplaceable experience in liturgical design, preparation, and performance. Among those to whom I owe the most are: Stephen Abbott, Joan Carruth, Ian Corrigan, Sharon Devlin, Sally Eaton, Rusty Elliot, Magenta Griffiths, Anodea Judith, Charles Hixson, Robert Larson, Deborah Lipp, Shirin Morton, Diana Paxson, Larry Press, and Selene Vega.

For editorial suggestions, I'm indebted to my former spouse Deborah Lipp and my current spouse Phaedra Heyman Bonewits.

Preface

Liturgies: The Good, the Bad, and the Annoying

It's Friday evening service at the Summerlands Pagan Center. The High Priestess has cast the circle, waving the sword in her hands up and down as she tries to fit the thirty people filling the twelve-foot-square room inside the ritual circle, which is looking more like an oval than anything else. The High Priest forgets his lines and has to consult the sacred cue-cards. Then the High Priestess insists, as she always does, on screeching out her favorite chant in the key of ouch, "We alllll come from the Gawd-ess! Annnd to Herrr we shall reee-turn…" It's going to be a long ceremony.

It's a beautiful summer night with a full moon shining overhead. In a hidden clearing in the middle of the woods, a dozen naked men and women are dancing on either side of you in the moonlight. Everyone whirls around the bonfire, singing and chanting the praises of the Moon Goddess and the Horned God of the Woods. The priest begins to invoke the power of the Goddess into the body of the priestess. Soon the Lady herself will speak to her people, and the dancing and feasting will go on for hours. Laughing as you whirl, you wish it would go on forever.

It's Sunday at the local Unitarian Universalist Church. The minister's been lecturing for some time now, and it's all very interesting, but the giggling kids in the Religious Education room across the hall seem to be having a lot more fun. The opening music tape was nice, and the music committee finally agreed upon some hymns that folks will sing without argument, but none of the songs have much soul. People are fidgeting, waiting for the service to end so they can get to the coffee and cookies. A whoop from across the hall makes it definite—the kids are having a great time. You wonder if maybe you should volunteer to help with R.E. next season.

It's almost sunrise on the morning of the Summer Solstice. A long line of women and men in white robes are leading a colorfully dressed congregation down to the lakeside. They gather in a circle and some of them begin to play harps, flutes, and drums. Soon a chant of praise to the Earth Mother begins, with voices joining in an old folk harmony that raises goose bumps on your skin. Offerings of flowers, cornmeal, beer, and poetry are made to the spirits of the woods and the lake, to the ancestors, and to the Old Gods and Goddesses. The clergy start a call and response chant between themselves and the congregation, ending just as the sun rises over the pines. You feel as if you are a part of something very ancient yet always new, as your body, mind, and heart join in singing a song of joy and praise.

Why This Book?

This book has been in progress for many years, sparked by my early and subsequent experiences in attending and observing large group public religious rituals, of faiths both mainstream and minority. I saw just how wonderful some of them could be and how awful they usually were.

As a young, Roman Catholic altar boy I was astonished to see how the exact same words and motions could be utterly boring or totally electrifying, depending upon which priest was performing them. I also noticed this personal factor at the Protestant Christian, Jewish, Buddhist, and Neopagan rituals I later attended. Eventually I realized that the structure of the rituals—their liturgical design—along with many other elements, helped or impeded their clergy's efforts.

My studies of comparative religious beliefs and practices among ancient, primitive, and modern spiritual groups, both mainstream and minority, along with over thirty-five years of experience creating, attending, and leading ceremonies as a Neopagan priest and magician, have clarified for me what the major factors are that affect the design, preparation, and performance of effective public worship rituals or liturgies. In this work I hope to share the fruits of these years of research and experimentation.

This book is intended to make people familiar with the most important theoretical and practical aspects of creating public worship rituals with genuine power and predictable results.* Although my focus is on Neopagan ceremonies, most of what I have to say will be applicable to the liturgies being created and modified by a wide variety of other liberal religious traditions.

I expect most members of the Neopagan community will enjoy reading this book, since Neopagans will eagerly devour (and strenuously debate) any text that deals with improving their religious practice. Members of the women's spirituality movements, Earth-centered religious movements, and many New Age spiritual groups may find this work a challenge to their current methods and theories, yet may benefit from incorporating into their practice the basic ideas presented.

Large parts of this book will appeal to people who belong to magical, metaphysical, and religious groups with traditions of liberal intellectual interests, such as Theosophists, Rosicrucians, Freemasons, Liberal Catholics, and Eco-Catholics, as well as to members of the New Thought, Religious Science, and Unity movements. Even liturgists from the moderate religious mainstream will find a few new ideas in these pages. Unitarian Universalists, especially the members of the Covenant of Unitarian Universalist Pagans (CUUPS), may find herein many of the missing pieces of their liturgical puzzles.

---

* Private religious rituals, whether family-oriented or solitary, are not liturgies and therefore, although important, will have to wait for future books.

A Note on Usages

References to my other books, as well as major dictionaries consulted, will usually be abbreviated after their first use; see the section on abbreviations below for a list of these.

While I don't have time to correspond with readers, I am always open to suggestions and new information for future editions of this and my other works. Email may be sent to me ℅ my website: www.neopagan.net and "snail mail" via my publisher.

Abbreviations Used in This Work

Other Books by the Author

AT: Authentic Thaumaturgy

BEGD: Bonewits's Essential Guide to Druidism

BEGWW: Bonewits's Essential Guide to Witchcraft and Wicca

PM: The Pagan Man

RE: Real Energy

RM: Real Magic

Dictionaries

Chambers: Chambers Dictionary of Etymology

SOED: Shorter Oxford English Dictionary, Fifth Edition

Webster's: Webster's Third New International Dictionary, Unabridged

1
Defining Our Terms

The Importance of Clear Definitions

Words are the primary symbolic tool most people use to control both our internal environments (shaping our thoughts, organizing their logic, analyzing complex concepts, etc.) and our external environments (communicating requests, information, directions, and/or commands to other people). Even if you are considering only the psychological, social, and cultural power of words, it becomes obvious that the clarity of your vocabulary can have a major impact on your life and on the lives of those around you.

The more complex the subject area about which you are communicating, the more necessary it is that your language be as precise as possible, and that you make sure all parties concerned are using equivalent definitions for the words and phrases of most importance. The further you move from the concrete to the abstract, however, or from the physical to the nonphysical, the more difficult it is to communicate effectively and efficiently, because it becomes harder to point to something visible and say "that's what I'm talking about." This is why the technical language used by sociology, for example, is more vague than that used in biology or chemistry. If you begin to talk about art or music, the vocabulary for anything other than the physical objects involved (pigments, sheet music, etc.) becomes vague within the first five minutes or so.

So it should be obvious that discussing magic, religion, or any-thing else having to do with the interface between the physical and the nonphysical, is going to have to be done very carefully. There *is* an appropriate technical vocabulary for these fields, but unless every-one knows the definitions being used, communication is difficult or impossible. Unfortunately, most writers and teachers in these areas define their terms vaguely, at best. All too often, they define them in ways that are self-contradictory and/or in severe conflict with main-stream concepts of those words, without explaining why they are changing the meaning. Such definitional confusion is deadly to clear thinking and decision-making.

So while I know that many readers are anxious to get to the "good stuff," first we need to spend a few pages carefully defining the techni-cal terms I'll be using for the rest of this book. Even if you think that my definitions are incomplete or incorrect, at least you'll know what I'm talking about. That clear understanding is the ground upon which agreement or disagreement with any later point can be made.*

So in the following pages we'll take a look at some of the most important words that will be used throughout this book. Please bear with me—boring as some of this may seem, the information will open some golden locks to understanding the rest of the book.

A Garden of −Isms and −Ologies

Monotheism ("one deity") is what we call a religion in which the theo-logians claim that only one deity exists (theirs, of course), and that all

---

* I often encourage readers and students to investigate the etymological ori-gins and historical evolution of various technical terms. Such an approach can (a) provide us with clearer concepts of what our ancestors and/or predecessors meant by those terms; and thus (b) give us clues to the an-cient customs and attitudes associated with their use; and (c) enable us to overcome later (often theologically motivated) changes to their meanings. Certainly, controlling our own vocabulary is one way that members of any minority take back the power that has been stolen from them. Nonethe-less, such background material has been known to put my students to sleep, so I've moved it to the appendix at the back of the book.

other spirits claiming (or claimed) to be deities are actually demons in disguise. Pure monotheisms are very rare—not until modern times do any seem to have existed at all. What usually happens is that various divine relatives, angels, saints, and demons join the *One* God as a part of the mythology. Most of these entities are indistinguishable from the deities and lesser spirits of the polytheistic religions previously occupying the same territory, because most of these associated spirits *are* the gods, goddesses, and nature spirits from the previous religions (or current ones from neighboring cultures).

Authentic, pure monotheism occurs only after the magical technology in a given culture has become so incompetent that miracles don't happen anymore, intellectuals become completely materialistic, and nobody really believes in *any* deities as real personalities. The problem, of course, is that such systems of belief don't really count as religions anymore (see below), because their philosophical and ethical beliefs no longer have a magical system connected.

Duotheism[1] (two deities) is what Neopagans call a religion in which the duotheologians claim that there are two deities, usually of opposite gender, and that all other spirits are aspects or faces of these two, through a process known as *theocrasy*[2] (deity mingling). The best example of this in the modern West is Wicca (Neopagan Witchcraft),[3] in which the deities are called the Goddess and the God. Duotheism seems to be a compromise between polytheistic ideas and a monotheistic culture. In Wicca's case, it started out as a Westernization of Hindu Tantra and Shakti cults.[4]

Duotheism should *not* be confused with the similar word *dualism* (two sorts), which is a belief that all the spiritual forces of the universe(s) are split into The Forces of Good™ and The Forces of Evil™, who are constantly at war. Almost all monotheisms (except for the *very* modern ones) are actually dualistic polytheisms (see below).

As you may have guessed by now, *polytheism* (many deities) is the word for a religion in which there are many deities of varying power and importance, and usually many lesser spirits as well. Each separate group of devotees within a polytheistic culture may decide that its deity is the best one *for them,* but all accept the reality of the others as genuine deities.

Pantheism (deity is all) is the belief that God/dess or the Gods *are* everything (or that Nature is divine); while *panentheism* (deity is in all) is the belief that God/dess or the Gods are *in* everything (and vice versa). The distinction depends on whether you believe that the Divine is simply being present or that she/he/it/they is/are actively participating in physical reality.

Either of these may blend with *animism* (everything is alive and has a spirit) or *animatism* (everything is alive). The subtle difference between these two concepts is often blurred into a generalized belief that everything is alive and/or has a spirit—including rocks, rivers, and clouds (or computers, motorcycles, and sewing machines).

Theology is the term for the organized study of God (however defined) and *thealogy* for the study of Goddess(es). *Duotheology* means the study of the Goddess and God (and their incorporated gods and goddesses), while *polytheology* will naturally mean the study of multiple deities of both (or any) genders.

These terms can include all kinds of intellectual speculations about the nature of the deity (or deities) and his/her/its/their relations to the world in general and humans in particular. These fields of study attempt to generate rational explanations of religious doctrines, practices and beliefs. These rational explanations may or may not bear any connection to any religion as actually conceived and practiced by the majority of its members, but theologians often tend to prefer intellectualizing pretty theories rather than observing actual human (or divine) behavior.

Paleo-, Meso-, and Neopaganism

The history of the term *Pagan* is complex and during most of its history, the word was used as an insult. Leaving the details for Appendix A, I'll simply say here that to modern people who call ourselves Pagan, it's a general term for polytheistic, pantheistic, panentheistic, and animistic religions, old and new, as well as their members. That, however, is too broad a definition to be much help, so we use the pre-fixes of *paleo-* (old), *meso-* (middle), and *neo-* (new) Paganisms.

Paleopaganism[5] refers to the original tribal religions of Europe, Africa, Asia, the Americas, Oceania, and Australia, when they were (or, in rare cases, still are) practiced as intact belief systems. Of the so-called "Great Religions of the World," Vedism (early Hinduism), Taoism, and Shinto fall under this category.

Mesopaganism[6] is the word used for those religions founded as attempts to recreate, revive, or continue what their founders *thought of* as the Paleopagan ways of their ancestors (or predecessors), but which were heavily influenced (accidentally, deliberately or involuntarily) by the monotheistic and dualistic worldviews of Judaism, Christianity, and/or Islam.[7]

Examples of Mesopagan belief systems include Freemasonry, Rosicrucianism, Spiritualism, Druidism as practiced by the Masonic-influenced fraternal movements in Europe and the Celtic Isles, the many Afro-American faiths (such as Voudoun, Santeria, or Macumba), Sikhism, and several sects of Hinduism that have been influenced by Islam and/or Christianity. Many liberal religious movements, such as Christian Science, New Thought, Unity, etc., can be thought of as Mesopagan, although their founders and some current members might be horrified to think so.

Neopaganism[8] refers to those religions created since 1940 or so (though they had literary roots going back to the mid-1800s), that have attempted to blend what their founders perceived as the best aspects of different types of Paleopaganism with modern Aquarian Age ideals, while consciously striving to eliminate as much as possible of the traditional Western monotheism and dualism.

These terms do not mark clear-cut categories. Historically, there are often periods, whether of decades or centuries, when Paleopaganism is changing into Mesopaganism, or Mesopaganism into Neopaganism. Furthermore, the founders and members of Mesopagan or Neopagan groups frequently prefer to believe (or at least declare) that they are being genuinely Paleopagan in their beliefs and practices. This myth of continuity (as anthropologists call it) is in keeping with the habits of most founders and members of new religions throughout human existence.

My own background as a Neopagan is rooted in my studies of Druidism, Wicca/Witchcraft, and Asatru (or Norse Paganism), as well as my experiences in Voodoo and Santeria. My opinions have been heavily influenced by folkloric and anthropological studies in world religions, modern occult and parapsychological research, and my participation in the evolution of the American Neopagan movement.[9]

Some Mystical Terms

The word *psychic* (mind or soul) is used by modern occultists, magicians, parapsychologists, and polytheologians to refer to rare or seldom-used powers of the mind, which are capable of causing effects that appear to contradict the mainstream world view of western science and philosophy. This is the way we'll use it in this book.

Modern psychologists, by the way, still use the word "psychic" to refer to all sorts of mental activities, including the perception and/or manifestation of Jungian archetypes of the collective unconscious. The term *psychic talent* is used to refer to abilities such as telepathy, clairvoyance, psychokinesis, precognition, the antipsi powers, and so forth.[10]

I'll be using the word *magic* quite a bit in this book, so the reader should understand that I'm not talking about wiggling your nose and having impossible things happen for (or to) you. My usual three formal definitions are listed in Appendix A, but for now only the third one is relevant: magic is a collection of rule-of-thumb techniques designed to get your psychic talents (whichever ones you happen to have) to do more or less what you want them to, more often than not, you hope. As such, it can be considered an artform as much as it is anything else, and that's the aspect of it we'll be emphasizing in this book.

There are two major flavors of magic, which I usually call *thaumaturgy* and *theurgy*. As I use the word, thaumaturgy is *magic that is done for mundane or secular purposes,* such as making rain come or go, healing the sick, or improving the fertility of the crops. A given magical act may be thaumaturgical even though it is done within a religious context, such as invoking a rain deity. I use the word theurgy to refer to *magic done for religious and/or psychotherapeutic purposes,* in order to attain salvation, empowerment, personal growth, etc., and/or to strengthen the Goddesses and Gods by giving them mana (see below), and/or to simply experience a sense of oneness with a chosen deity or the cosmos as a whole. These two words simply indicate opposite ends of a continuous range of activity and intent. Locating the exact place upon that spectrum that a proposed use of psychic/spiritual/magical energy belongs is an important part of ceremonial planning, whether liturgical or not.

The word *spirit* is used for all sorts of nonphysical beings, including those living inside people, which are often called souls. The word *spiritual* is one of those marvelously vague terms that means whatever the user of it wants it to, at the moment he or she uses it. Most people today think of spiritual things (!) as being those that make you a better person, usually from an ethical or moral point of view. Today the field of psychology has taken over much of what used to be considered the realm of the spiritual, and terms like "personal growth," "maturity," and "self-actualization" are more likely to be used by liberal theologians than phrases like "spiritual" are.

We should remember that the root concept of spiritual has to do with spirits—that is, beings without bodies, no matter how a given (poly) theological system may define them, and regardless of their moral qualities. So activities and ideas that deal with interactions between humans and spirits can technically be considered spiritual, whether we agree with the moral content of those interactions or not. However, most of the time in this book we will use the word in its modern blend of religious, moral, and psychotherapeutic meanings.

The energies used in ESP, psychokinesis, and other psychic talents are essentially the same as the magical energies used in casting spells.[11] I usually call these energies *mana,* a word that the Paleopagan inhabitants of Hawaii, Tahiti, and New Zealand apparently used to refer to energies that westerners might label under varying circumstances with terms such as spiritual, magical, psychic, psychological, artistic, vital, numinous, charismatic, etc. In most cases, the Oceanic term is used to refer to dynamic energies that enable achievement of various goals—that is to say, "power, power, wonder-working power!"

I believe mana not only permeates every human, but the entire universe as well, since I suspect it is part of the structure of reality, like electromagnetism or gravity. Perhaps it's what physicists call dark energy (because it's invisible) or even the quantum field beneath all matter and energy.[12] This fits well with Neopagan concepts of divinity as both transcendent and immanent. I further believe that deities and all other spirits are either composed of mana or at least require it to communicate with humans.[†]

Religion and Ritual

To an occultist (a student of that which is occult or hidden), a *religion* is a magical system that has been combined with a philosophical and ethical system, usually oriented toward supernatural beings.[13] It's possible, although difficult, to have a magical system that is not part of a religion. Such a system requires the belief that the people doing the magic are only bringing into operation some occult controlling principle of nature, rather than invoking spirits, however, to have a growing, powerful, attractive religion without some sort of magical system (whether or not it's ever called such) seems to be impossible. To a Neopagan, a religion is also a psychic structure, network, or organism composed of the shared beliefs, experience, and related habits of *all* the members, not just the (poly)theologians, of any group calling itself a religion.

The word *worship* has an enormous amount of emotional baggage attached to it, so we need to be very careful in how we use it. Again leaving the linguistic details for Appendix A, we can say that it's primary meaning is to show honor and affection for something or

---

† See chapter 2 of this book, The Nature of Deities and Vice Versa.

someone, especially in religious acts or rituals. Whether you are worshipping a spirit, an ancestor, or a deity, you are showing them (and any observers who may be present) that you have respect for them. You are acknowledging that their status is greater than yours in some fashion, and perhaps most important in a polytheological sense, you are showing your affection as well as reverence for them.

A *ritual* or *rite* is any ordered sequence of events, actions, and/or directed thoughts, especially one that is meant to be repeated in the same manner each time, that is designed to produce and manage one or more *altered states of consciousness* (ASCs) within which certain results may be obtained.[14]

As Phaedra puts it:

> Well-executed ritual contains a sequence of *managed* ASCs appropriate to both their place in the sequence and the overall goal at hand. The activities and techniques (smudging, centering, circumambulation, vocalization, movement, etc.) are ordered in such a way as to more and more *focus our attention* to the work at hand (i.e., *alter us from everyday consciousness* to an ASC that will allow us to *do* the magick). A good ritual will reach its peak of focus and intensity at the power moment and then, in steps, return us to normal everyday consciousness.[15]‡

The results may be mundane, as in achieving efficiency at your job through the ingestion of coffee in order to alter your state of consciousness to awake, and thus to facilitate the accomplishment of your morning tasks.§

The desired results may instead be intellectual ones, as with the discoveries made through the various rituals known as "the scientific method." Or they might be artistic, as in the ritual called "Beethoven's Ninth Symphony." They might be psychological, as in the repetitive

---

‡ But see Chapter 9, Masculine vs. Feminine Spell/Prayer Casting.

§ This is known as the worship of Caffeina, Goddess of Awareness, as practiced by the Javacrucian Order (revealed to the outer world in 1974 by my first wife Rusty Elliott and myself).

behavior of people suffering from obsessive-compulsive disorder, but for the purposes of this book, we'll restrict the use of the word "ritual" to refer to those that are designed to produce various magical, psychic, and/or spiritual results.

One primary purpose of ritual is to reduce uncertainty, through the conscious or subconscious use of established patterns of behavior that are known to have worked in the past, and which are (by the magical Law of Pragmatism[16]) therefore considered to be true, correct, or effective. The more people who are involved in attempting to accomplish a given goal, whether pulling in a fishing-net or beseeching the gods for rain, the more useful ritual behavior becomes for coordinating their actions.

Ritual is often confused with *ritualism,* which (like many other –isms) consists of an obsession with the superficial aspects of the root word (originally it just meant the use of ritual). Dry and sterile rituals performed by clergy and congregations who have forgotten the reasons behind their actions, but who are sticklers for tradition, have given an undeservedly bad name to ritual. Today's Neopagans are reclaiming ritual as a positive term.

Ritual is often practiced by people who don't call it that—even in religious circumstances. Members of some liberal religions might, for example, say "We don't do rituals in our church/ fellowship/temple. We just have a standard order of service that we do every week."¶

The word *ceremony* originally referred to public rituals of a sacred nature (see below). Some use the word to imply a ritual whose sacred or historical meaning has been lost, and which is now only an empty show. This meaning is especially popular among members of some liberal religions who consider all ritual as just-empty-ritual (said very quickly as if all one word). However, ceremony is usually now used as a synonym for ritual in general, both by the mainstream western culture and within the Neopagan community. So you can assume that ceremony equals ritual equals rite for the rest of this book.

¶ They may not call it a ritual but god(s) help you if you try to change anything in it!

Liturgy

Finally—we get to the key word for this book. *Liturgy* means group rituals of religious worship, especially public ones. Every religion in the world has some sort of these; plain or fancy, noisy or quiet, in large groups or small. It seems to be a natural human instinct to join with others to express our hopes and fears, thoughts and aspirations, and to connect with whatever we perceive deity to be. Why is it that so many modern religious ceremonies are so disappointing to their participants, when the ancient ones, or those now being practiced by "primitive" tribes and members of "weird" religions, seem to be so much more satisfying?

The answers lie in *liturgics,* the field of study and practice that deals with the design, preparation, and performance of public worship ceremonies. This is a field usually pursued exclusively by professional clergy and theologians, despite the fact that everyone who ever attends a religious ritual has an interest in what is happening and why. Religious elites often consider liturgy to be strictly an intellectual exercise and spend their time coming up with philosophical and theological justifications for what are in reality their own tribal traditions. In the process, they appear to many observers to have drained the life out of their liturgies and put the spirits of their members into ceremonial straitjackets.

Ancient and modern tribal peoples, on the other hand, were and are fully aware that creating powerful and effective worship ceremonies requires art and philosophy, magic and mysticism, drama and movement. Their shamans, medicine people, priestesses, and drummers know far more about what makes a religious ceremony satisfying than the traditional Western liturgists do.

Neopagans have been learning for the last sixty years how to combine this tribal wisdom with the intellectual and experimental traditions of the western occult movements (and modern parapsychology) to improve the chances of having rituals that can actually produce observable changes in the physical world, in addition to helping us with our personal growth. As a result, the average Neopagan liturgy is far more exciting and satisfying to its participants than the rituals of the religious mainstream seem to be to theirs.

For a religion to remain healthy, its ceremonies, both public and private, need to be physically, mentally, emotionally, and spiritually satisfying, with a strong sense of mystery and magic to them. Liturgies that are missing these vital elements are crippled, if not dead, and will eventually drive their participants into a state of spiritual paralysis or force them to abandon their faith in order to find one with satisfying worship ceremonies. Thus, liturgy is one of the most important aspects of any religion, and improving the quality of liturgical experience is an essential task for all those concerned about the health and future of their faith.

As we will see, a liturgy can be thought of as a worship ritual composed of a series of mini-rituals, each intended to produce a specific altered state of consciousness that accomplishes a particular task, and each leading smoothly into the next ASC and the next task. Nonetheless, to avoid boredom—or at least minimize it!—the terms liturgy, ritual, rite, and ceremony will be used as synonyms throughout. Now let's begin our exploration of Neopagan liturgics with some basic polytheology!

2

THE POLYTHEOLOGY
OF WORSHIP

A WARNING

This book may upset a few professional theologians, whether liberal, conservative, mainstream, or New Age (not to mention thealogians), so I should probably point out why I have chosen to deliberately ignore several philosophical and theological issues that many theologians might consider essential to any study of liturgy.

Many theologians have the bad habit of assuming that their rational, abstract view of their religion *is* their religion, thus confusing their intellectual map with the living territory. To magicians and Neopagans, however, a religion is (among many other things) a psychic structure composed of the beliefs of *all* of its followers, not just the theologians. In fact, the opinions of theologians are often irrelevant to the real magical and spiritual power of a religion.

In any event, the ideas and opinions expressed in this book are based on observations of the ways that people (mortal or immortal) *actually believe and behave* in their religious rituals, as distinct from the ways that some theologians/thealogians might think they should. I use this approach because I find the disciplines of anthropology, sociology of religion, and parapsychology of much greater use for understanding liturgy than philosophy ever is.

Since the 1960s, modern science has tended more and more toward multi-model, pluralistic theories that fit very well indeed with polytheism and traditional non-monotheistic occultism. So it is especially sad that even people who have consciously rejected conservative religious beliefs are reluctant to let go of certain scientistic prejudices. *Scientism,* also known as "Scientolatry," is the worship of the obsolete scientific paradigm of a dead, mechanistic universe.*

Magic as *magic,* as a way of causing measurable and observable changes in the physical universe, collides head-on with scientistic dogmas about the nature of reality. Most people simply don't have the intellectual courage to deal with multiple levels of reality, paradoxes, or complex ambiguity. They like things kept as simple as possible, so they wind up closing their eyes to the complicated, yet potentially liberating, aspects of their environment.

Modern religious ceremonies, both Neopagan and mainstream, are affected by this mainstream scientistic bias for similar reasons. If you don't believe that your deities are real people, in *some* sense or another, then the concept of worship becomes meaningless. As the ancient Roman author Seneca put it, "The first way to worship the Gods is to believe in the Gods."[17]

The Nature of Deities and Vice Versa

But who and what *are* the Gods? The simplest and most common theory about the Goddesses and Gods is that they are powerful spiritual or supernatural beings who are somehow not limited by the currently accepted laws of Nature. This simple theory says that deities are very powerful people who just don't happen to have physical bodies, except when they want to. Some of them are probably the ancestors of the tribe, possibly even the creator(s) of the physical world. They have very strong magical powers, which they can use to help or hurt mortals. These ideas frequently go along with a concept of a *spiritual*

---

* See *Real Energy*, Appendix C.

hierarchy of greater and lesser gods and goddesses, nature spirits, ancestors, elementals, demons, etc.

Some atheistic or agnostic theories attempt to explain (away) deities and other spirits as merely culturally transmitted memories of dead heroes and magicians,[18] or as memories of visitors from other cultures or even other planets (the "Ancient Astronauts" theory[19]), or as necessary fictional characters in culturally useful ritual dramas (based on the idea that ritual creates mythology more often than vice versa), or even as mistakes in folk etymology.[20]

Those who don't believe in the existence of anything supernatural, and who define deity solely in the monotheistic sense of that which is supremely supernatural, will often conclude that deities don't exist. They are in essence saying, "If I can't have the monotheistic God, I won't have any at all." This is ironic, considering that most atheists, agnostics, and humanists don't consciously acknowledge that they are still letting the monotheistic theologians define their terms for them.

Psychologists differ in their approach to this topic. Some consider deities to be memories of infantile fantasies of omnipotence (usually adding a snide comment about "magical thinking"). Others stress childhood memories of all-powerful parents. The Jungians offer the insights of most value to practicing occultists and Neopagans, with theories about the collective unconscious and its archetypes.

Jung's ideas of the collective unconscious, St. Pierre Teilhard De Chardin's concept of the "Noesphere," my theory of the "Switchboard"[21] (as a telepathic network of all living people), and even the Theosophist's "causal plane," are all concepts pointing in the same direction. No matter what terminology we prefer, it's possible to think of deities and other spirits as being energy patterns within some sort of a psychic network that connects all humanity.

We can theorize that when one of these energy patterns gets enough mana fed into it, it begins to act more and more independently, and to engage in behavior designed to encourage more mana to be fed to it (if it just steals mana when it wants to, it will be called a demon or evil spirit). If a spirit gets to be large and powerful enough, and is perceived as predominately beneficial, it may become something that people will call a deity. A feedback loop is established between the deity and his/her worshipers through mythology, ritual, the arts, polytheology, and psychic phenomena.

Regardless of the metaphor we choose, I think that deities and other spirits either exist within this psychic network or, at the very least, communicate with humans through it (from wherever else they may be). As my Druidic path expresses it, this *Otherworld,* together with the *Three Worlds* (Land, Waters, and Sky) lived in by humans, animals, and plants, constitutes a universal ecosystem that includes all of the Earth Mother's children, physical and nonphysical.[22]

To study the nature of worship, it's only necessary to consider two basic ideas: First, that a god or goddess is (among other things) *a pattern of energy,* regardless of whether you refer to that energy as psychological, cultural, magical, psychic, spiritual, or anything else. Second, while anthropomorphic deity descriptions can be deadly when applied to supposedly Supreme Beings (see next section), we should still be able to appreciate them as—if nothing else—useful metaphors to describe the types of interactions appropriate for humans to have with deities.

No matter what deities and other spirits may really be in some abstract objective universe, in the subjective personal multiverse in which we experience our daily lives, these energy patterns frequently act *as if* they were real people, of various sizes and powers, who just don't happen to have physical bodies as we generally conceive of them. Polytheists are free to accept a multimodel theory that involves all these possible explanations, and many more besides.

But What About the Supreme Being?

You'll notice that this discussion has pretty much ignored the standard monotheistic idea of deity as meaning (only) a Supreme Being. That's because I believe that such an entity is beyond the ability of human language to discuss meaningfully—as soon as theologians start talking about "infinite this" and "omni- that" they begin tying themselves into logical knots. Worse, when the logical paradoxes of infinity are applied to ethical and moral issues, sanctified atrocities are the usual result (burning a heretic at the stake, for example, because half an hour of flaming agony is nothing compared to an eternity of assumed hellfire).

Infinity-talk almost always leads to dualism as well, since a God who is both infinitely good and infinitely powerful requires an infinitely evil (and infinitely powerful) Devil (or Antigod) to account for the presence of evil in the world. Indeed, the only practical solution to the classic "Problem of Evil" in monotheistic theology, as Harold Kushner pointed out,[23] is to reduce some of the ascribed infinities down to a rational size, thus returning the One God to his original role as just another tribal deity.

Anything powerful enough to have created billions of galaxies, each with billions of stars (and at least a few million planets with the potential for intelligent, nonhuman life) is unlikely to have any motivations, goals, or needs that a human being is likely to understand. From a Neopagan viewpoint, she/he/it is thus an inappropriate subject for worship, and doesn't require much space in a book about liturgy. The deities associated with our planet, on the other hand, *are* appropriate for humans to worship.

Ben Franklin had some wise things to say about all this back in 1728:

> I imagine it great vanity in me to suppose that the Supremely Perfect does in the least regard such an inconsiderable nothing as man. More especially, since it is impossible for me to have any positive clear idea of that which is infinite and incomprehensible, I cannot conceive otherwise than that He, the Infinite Father, expects or requires no worship or praise from us, but that He is even infinitely above it.[24]

I know that there are many good people who regularly engage in worship ceremonies that they *believe to be* directed toward a Supreme Being. However, if you examine their words and actions carefully, you will usually find that they are instead worshipping tribal deities who have been inflated in the minds of their worshippers to the rank of a Supreme Being.

The Worship Bargain

Most Paleo- and Neopagans believe(d) that the gods need us as much as we need the gods. Every time you have a thought about a deity, you feed mana into that deity's energy pattern. If a lot of people think frequently about a particular deity, she or he can become very powerful indeed. It's as if everyone were making spiritual deposits in Mt. Olympus Savings and Loan. Every once in a while, to assist with the survival of his/her worshippers (and thus his/her own survival), or simply to encourage more mana to be deposited, a deity may decide (or be persuaded by a magician/clergyperson) to pay interest or dividends on those deposits of mana. This often takes the form of divine energy being given to or through a clergyperson to be used for magical or religious purposes, though sometimes the deity may simply release some of her/his/its power to an individual worshipper in the form of inspirations, personal spiritual strengthening, or actual miracles.

This reciprocal relationship of "we scratch their auras, they scratch ours," is known as *the worship bargain*. It may not sound very spiritual to modern Westerners, but billions of Paleopagans for tens of thousands of years have considered it spiritual enough.

Remember, when you are worshipping a spirit, an ancestor, or a deity, you are showing them (and perhaps any observers who may be present) that you have respect for them. From a Paleo- or Neopagan point of view, worship also involves feeding mana to the deities or other spirits, as well as establishing a personal relationship with whoever is being worshipped.

Nothing in the nature of worship requires groveling, abasement, or self-humiliation. Those negative concepts have become part of our Western view of worship because of conservative monotheistic ideas about a Supreme Being who supposedly demands self-denigrating behavior from his worshippers. With such a deity concept, worship ceases to be an act of interdependence between mortals and their divinities, and instead becomes a process in which each mortal tries desperately to prove his or her worthiness to receive love and blessings from the Supreme Being.

It seems to me that if there is a Supreme Being, and if she/he/it is interested in interacting with mortals on one planet circling a third-rate star in one of the lesser galaxies in this corner of the cosmos, then she/he/it is going to bestow love and blessings on *everyone* who is open to receive them—and I suspect that most mainstream liberal theologians would agree with me. Nonetheless, this idea of divine love as something that has to be earned by having a low self-image has polluted many mainstream religions.

One of the main differences between Neopaganism and many forms of Paleopaganism (and those mainstream religions) is that our worship of the goddesses and gods is seldom motivated by fear. Psychologically, this is probably because we, like the liberal mainstream religions, live in much safer and more secure times than our ancestors did. Also, since Neopagan polytheologies have no concept of original sin, we don't live in constant worry about offending our deities. Thus, we have no need, as a general rule, to propitiate our deities by giving them bribes to buy forgiveness, nor do we fear divine punishment for normal desires and actions. A deity may give one of us a spiritual "spanking" now and then, but such negative feedback never descends to the sort of divine child abuse so common in other religions.

The concept of *immanence*—that deity(ies) is/are inside us as much as, or more than, she/he/it/they is/are outside of us—is important here. The Church of All Worlds, the first group to use the term Neo-Pagan in our community,[25] also popularized the phrase "Thou art God"[26] and later, "Thou art Goddess" (or "God/dess"). From this the idea developed that if the gods and goddesses we worship are within us, and we are their children, then we must be godlings. So we had better start taking our share of divine responsibility for fixing up the planet. When we grow up in a few—or a few hundred—lifetimes, perhaps we will become full-fledged deities ourselves (an idea in keeping with both Voudoun and Hindu theories of deity).

Neopagan relationships with our divine parents, then, tend to be less like those of a terrified six-year-old, and more like those of a teenager who knows that mom and dad really do love him/her and are willing to allow a reasonable amount of well-intentioned experimentation.†

Westerners who have lived through the latter half of the twentieth century have had more choices about almost every aspect of their lives than any previous generation in human history. Nuclear weapons and ecological disasters have made it very clear that we must choose wisely, and that there is a price to be paid for every choice made.

The new science of ecology has reminded us of what our ancestors once knew intuitively: everything in the world is connected to everything else, often in subtle and mysterious ways (this is true even on the subatomic level of reality, as shown by the concept of "quantum entanglement"—see *RE*).[27] All of Nature is checks and balances. To gain a desired advantage, you must usually sacrifice something else.

If you want to get ahead in your chosen career, you may have to sacrifice sleeping late. If you want to learn to play the violin, you may have to sacrifice the hours you might otherwise spend watching television. If you want your grandchildren to live to adulthood, you *will* have to give up some of your leisure time and start working to achieve that goal.

So Neopagans give sacrifices to our deities, knowing that the exchanges involved in the worship bargain are examples of just such choices being made.‡

Invocation and Evocation

The words *invocation* and *evocation* refer to two of the ways in which humans may communicate with deities or other spirits. Unfortunately, the terms are often confused with each other. The magical Law of

---

† But first clean up your room!
‡ See Chapter 9, Sacrifices.

Evocation states: "It is possible to establish *external* communication with entities from either inside or outside of oneself, said entities seeming to be *outside* of oneself during the communication process." The magical Law of Invocation, in contrast, says: "It is possible to establish *internal* communication with entities from either inside or outside of oneself, said entities seeming to be *inside* of oneself during the communication process."[28]

What's important to remember about invocation and evocation is that although exactly the same psychic/magical/spiritual processes *may* be involved, the perceptions of the participants are different. Evocation as a magical technique is most associated in the West with the Renaissance ceremonial magicians, who drew magical circles to protect themselves, and magical triangles outside of these to contain the entities they called daemons (neutral spirits), demons (evil spirits), angels (good spirits), elementals (personifications of the classical four elements of Air, Earth, Fire, and Water), etc. These entities would seem to appear in the triangles at a physical and psychological distance from the magician, enabling him to communicate with them safely. Some modern occultists believe that ceremonial magic is a form of psychotherapy, designed so that a magician can deal with his personal traumas (internal demons) at a safe psychological distance.[29]

Invocation, on the other hand, is an internalized rather than externalized activity. Divine or other spiritual energies are communed with inside the invoker's own psyche. Prayers that are traditionally labeled invocations are designed to encourage spirits to communicate through the processes known as *inspiration, conversation, channeling* (formerly called mediumship), and *possession*. These are not distinct phenomena, but rather steps along a continuous range of experiential intensity.

A deity may choose to inspire (literally, "breathe through") the invoker with thoughts, images, and words—perhaps to be shared with a group. Or she or he may decide to converse with an invoker in an entirely internal manner, with only the invoker "hearing" the deity's words. If the deity wishes to share more information or power, and the invoker is properly prepared, the deity's words and/or mana may be channeled directly through the invoker's mouth or body. If the mana channeling is perceived as happening outside the body of the clergyperson, magician, or psychic (such as into a cup of wine or some magical or religious tool), this can be called *evocatory channeling* rather than invocatory. When mediumship becomes stronger and the deity decides to partially or completely take over the body of the invoker (suppressing or displacing the consciousness of the invoker) this sharing of divine power becomes a possession experience.

Although spiritual conversation and inspiration happen frequently in Neopagan liturgy, and channeling happens now and then, full-scale divine possessions are extremely rare, as they are in most Western religions. The Afro-American Mesopagan faiths such as Santeria and Voudoun, as well as their charismatic Christian offshoots, have possession by their Holy Spirit(s) on a regular basis, and their magical techniques would be well worth studying for those who desire this degree of intensity in their liturgies—or who wish to avoid it!

3

A Common Worship Pattern

Five Phases of Liturgy

In order to understand the discussions in the rest of this book, it will help to have a framework within which later comments about specific liturgical activities can be placed. Some of this chapter will only make full sense after you have read the rest of the book, but please have patience. By the time we reach the end, it will all tie together.

If you analyze the public worship rituals of those cultures still maintaining a strong belief in the existence and power of the deity(ies) they worship, *and* still practicing (however unconsciously) a working magical system associated with public worship, you will notice strong similarities in their liturgical designs.[30] Among the Indo-European influenced religions, for example,[31] there is a commonly found pattern that consists of five main sequences or phases of activity which occur in this order:

Phase One: Consecrating time and space, and getting the people purified, centered, grounded, and unified into a group mind. This makes them ready for...

Phase Two: Re-creating the cosmos by defining a ritual center and/or opening the *Gates Between the Worlds*, enumerating the various parts of existence and (usually) evoking or invoking entities from them, thus starting a *back and forth* flow of mana through the gates, culminating with...

Phase Three: Giving the major part of the congregation's mana *to* the primary deity(ies) being worshipped on the occasion. This is followed by...

Phase Four: Receiving and using a return flow of mana *from* the primary deity(ies) of the occasion; and finally...

Phase Five: Reversing the beginnings of the rite (unwinding the various mana fields woven) and closing the ceremony down.

There are also additional steps that take place immediately before and after the performance of each liturgy, but these are usually not thought of as part of it by the average attendee.

Please note what I am *not* saying here. I am *not* saying that these phases (and the steps within each that I will discuss) are the only way to do effective liturgy. I *am* saying that if you carefully examine the liturgical designs of successful worship rituals you are likely to find this pattern being used, however unconsciously, as the underlying organic structure.

Specific liturgies may skip steps, or merge them, or do them in a different order than that presented here or in my other writings. The reader should take these differences as opportunities for meditation and/or experimentation.

Now, let's take a look at these phases and their steps in some useful detail.

Preliminary Steps

These preliminary steps are fairly obvious and every religion has them: baths and other purifications done by the clergy; prayers and meditations before the rite begins; special blessings of the altar and its tools; special dressing and/or prayers by the congregation before arrival; last minute instructions to the participants, etc. Some of these steps may be done during phase one as part of creating sacred space and time, but most are done beforehand for practical magical and mundane reasons.*

Phase One: Starting the Rite
The Clear-Cut Beginning: Consecration of Time

Every ritual, whether religious or not, should have a clearly designated beginning. This can be signaled by a bell ringing, by the clergy showing up in full regalia, by candles (or a chalice in Unitarian Universalist rites!) being lit, or in some other fashion. What's important is that the participants receive the cue telling their subconscious minds the ceremony is starting.

One of the primary purposes of religious ritual (most of phase two in this discussion) is to *re-create the cosmos* and thus to assert and reinforce our ideas about reality and meaning. The declaration of sacred time returns us to when the deity(ies) first made the cosmos (however our culture or subculture may conceive of it and them). As Mircea Eliade puts it:

> *By its very nature, sacred time is reversible* in the sense that, properly speaking, it is *a primordial mythical time made present.* Every religious festival, any liturgical time, represents the re-actualization of a sacred event that took place in a mythical past, "in the beginning"... Man *[sic]* desires to recover the active presence of the Gods; he also desires to live in the world as it came from the Creator's hands, fresh, pure, and strong.[32]

When we declare time to be sacred, we are declaring our intent and ability to return to those thrilling days of yesteryear, when the world was new, the animals could talk, and deities were seen everywhere. We step outside of normal, mundane, or secular time and into eternity.

---

* See Chapter 11.

The Consecration of Space

Having begun with the consecration of time, you immediately need to consecrate a bit of space. In a place normally used for religious activities, all you need to do is walk into the temple or grove with a proper intent, and the sacred nature of the place will become activated (that is, you'll notice it). In a location that is not normally viewed as sacred, you'll need to mark the perimeter of the area you plan to use. This can be done *loosely* by having a procession go around the area, or (if you're short on maneuvering room) by having everyone hold hands while singing a song or chant about sacred space (and time, if possible, to reinforce that consecration).

The perimeter of your ritual area can also be set up *tightly* by physically marking the edges of the area, followed by ritually consecrating those edges. The choice of a loose or tight boundary depends upon the precise kind of magical/religious activity you intend to do. More specifically, it depends on how critical it is to keep certain types of mana in or out of the working area, either temporarily or permanently. Either way, the re-creation of the cosmos requires that the chaos of mundane space be symbolically kept at a distance for the duration.

Purification of the People and Site

Most religions will pause at this point to bless the participants and/or to purify them in some fashion if this wasn't done before the ritual.[†] Most Paleo- and Neopagans don't have a myth of original sin (although Neopagans generally approve of originality), so they don't try to cleanse the participants from some sort of innate evil, but rather to help them to focus on the events at hand by clearing away all irrelevant or incompatible thoughts.

If you had been cooking an Indian curry, and then decided to bake an apple pie for dessert, you would naturally wash any lingering curry powder off your hands before starting to cut up the apples. If you

---

† See Chapter 11, Ceremonial Baths.

were a doctor who had been working with disease victims and then had to attend someone else with open wounds, you would make sure that your hands were thoroughly sterile before touching her. If you had been doing a weather spell, and your mind was full of low pressure zones, jet streams, and cirrus cloud formations, and you then desired to do a fertility spell for the crops, you would need to clear your mind of all those weather-oriented thoughts before attempting to get fertile.

In the first two examples, neither curry powder nor microbes are necessarily evil (though some would argue about either), but their leftover presence could cause the results of your later activities to be less than satisfactory. The washing of hands can be a powerful symbolic act, so it should come as no surprise to know that many cooks and surgeons make a much bigger fuss over cleaning themselves than either the culinary or the medical arts require.

In the third example, again, what you want to get rid of is not evil, wicked, or sinful, just inappropriate. Here a physical cleansing of your self (and the working area and tools) becomes more obviously symbolic. As in other rituals, what you are doing is giving your subconscious a series of cues, in this case to wipe your internal blackboard clean so that you can start writing new thoughts upon it.

Obviously, someone who feels that she/he does not belong there because they have done something wrong will need special attention. Purification from tainted mana (but not from moral responsibility to make amends) would then be appropriate. Hunters, for example, who had just slaughtered animals they considered their four-footed siblings, would want to be cleansed from their "blood guilt" (that's the usual anthropological term) before rejoining the tribe's ceremonies.

Similarly, a special blessing may often be done on the physical area where the liturgy is to take place. This reinforces the concepts of sacred space and time in the minds of the participants, and can magically *charge* an area to more effectively control the expected flows of mana. An actual exorcism of the ritual area shouldn't be necessary, especially outdoors (unless you forgot to check out the vibes of the place first). But if you or someone else has been doing magical or religious rituals (or any activity for that matter) of an incompatible sort in the same location recently, you'll want to psychically clean the area, either along with an earlier physical cleansing or else at this point of the liturgy.

There are a wide variety of ways to exorcise an area; you should choose a style that fits with the rest of the ceremony. Most of the time, your exorcism should focus on the idea of cleaning and tidying up, rather than driving demons out (there aren't that many demons around anyway). You may want, however, to take this opportunity to set up *wards* (psychic defenses) around the site to prevent disturbance by unfriendly mortals, should that be a matter of concern.

Centering, Grounding, Linking, and Merging

Centering is a term used in Neopagan and New Age ritual technique to refer to each person finding the center of awareness within him/herself. If you close your eyes and say to yourself, "Where am I in this body, anyway?" some people will find their center behind their eyes, some in their heart area, some in their belly, and some elsewhere. There is no right or wrong place for your center to be (at least not for the purposes of most ceremonies) from a polytheological aspect. However, from a movement-awareness viewpoint, you might be better off to move your center of awareness to the solar plexus region, tuck your pelvis under, and otherwise stand or sit in a fully relaxed manner, in order to open your body up for the maximum internal flow of mana.

Grounding, on the other foot, is one of those technical terms that is commonly used for two very different ideas. The first is to make a physical and psychic connection to the ground, both as a source of physical and psychological stability, and as a source of mana from the Earth Mother. The second is as an electromagnetic metaphor for draining off excess mana into the ground (or occasionally into your ceremonial tools) just as a lightning rod grounds electricity.

The Earth-connecting sense is the primary one at this point in most rituals. However, draining off excess mana may become equally important here if members of the group are overwhelmed with hard to handle emotions, especially unpleasant ones such as grief, anger, or fear. Then grounding becomes a matter of combining the two methods: entering the healing darkness of the Mother, discharging the excess emotional energy (mana), and being reborn as a stronger person, ready to continue.

The next step after grounding, regardless of which method you have chosen, is to psychically *link* (make direct connections) with the others present and then to *merge* into a *group mind*. That's a scary-sounding term, but it's probably just what Tom F. Driver in *Liberating Rites* (following Victor Turner in *The Ritual Process)*, calls *communitas*, a sacred recognition of community without hierarchy or social limits. Others use the term "group mind" to refer to a type of communal telepathy, in which each person has a direct psychic link to everyone else present. Think of it as getting everyone present on the same wavelength, experiencing the same emotions and seeing the same visual and mental images. Just as multiple musical instruments si-multaneously playing the same notes can produce resonant sounds, more powerful than the sum of their parts, so too, minds functioning in psychic resonance can produce much greater psychic power and control.

All this is usually done through guided meditation or prayers to encourage individual centering and grounding, followed by a remind-er to the congregation of what they have in common (ancestry, be-liefs, relations to the divine, etc.), and some sort of meditation, song, or other activity designed to promote a sense of unity and to begin the coordinated circulation of mana by the group.

Specification of the Ritual Purpose and Historical Precedent

Once the group mind has been created, it is reminded of the pur-pose of the ritual, which might be pure and simple worship, the cel-ebration of a holiday, an effort to bring rain or heal sickness, or any other purpose that the members of the group have agreed upon. This gives everyone the intellectual, artistic, magical, and spiritual themes they need to concentrate on during the course of the ceremony. With a small group, this step is easy to forget, since everybody already knows all this. Yet if one newcomer or unexpected guest attends, they can generate a lot of confusion in their ignorance.

Just as importantly, the members of the group mind are told that what they are doing is traditional, that it has been done before by their ancestors or predecessors. Often the ritual is said to have been invented by a deity, or to commemorate a deity's actions, during an especially sacred time (usually the creation of the world or the early years after it). The sacred time experienced by the participants in the sacred space is identified with the original sacred time. The universal human need to make this cosmic identification between the sacred space/time of the ritual and the sacred space/time of the creation of the world (or at least of one's sect) is a major reason why people will say pseudo-historical nonsense in their ceremonies. They're not consciously telling lies, exactly. They are living in mythic time, an experience that enables them to make necessary psychic connections to the collective unconscious, as well as providing a source of both power and self-confidence.

Specification of the Deity(ies) of the Occasion and Reasons for Choice

Next, the participants are reminded about the deity or deities who is/are to be the focus for that occasion, and of why the deity/deities chosen is/are appropriate. In a group that normally only worships one or two deities, this step can be very short, but in the more polytheistic ones it's important that everyone know which of several possible deities is/are the focus of worship for this particular event. Even in a duotheistic system, since both the Lord and the Lady have multiple names, particular "faces" or *aspects* need to be selected and the reasons for their choice explained.

PHASE TWO: RE-CREATING THE COSMOS

As Mircea Eliade repeatedly mentions in his many fine books, a central part of most religious rituals is re-creating the cosmos. Speaking of the ancient Vedic rituals, for example, he says, "Every sacrifice repeats the primordial act of creation and guarantees the continuity of the world for the following year."[33] *Cosmogonic* (worlds creating) aspects of liturgy are sometimes present just to commemorate the creation, but more often they are also meant to orient the ritual participants in relation to all the other parts of their universe and to all the other beings in it. Catholics, for example, will mention heaven and hell, angels, saints, devils, etc., and the deity(ies) to be worshipped. Norse Pagans might mention the Nine Worlds of the Norse cosmos and their inhabitants. Shamanistic rites would talk about the Celestial regions above and the Underworld below, listing the spirits to be found therein. In all cases, however, a necessary first step to re-creating the cosmos seems to be defining a ritual center, the place from which the *new* cosmos can be born.

Defining the Ritual Center and/or Evoking the Gatekeeper

For maximum effectiveness, most liturgies require a specifically defined *ritual center*. As Eliade puts it:

> ...for nothing can begin, nothing can be *done*, without a previous orientation—and any orientation implies acquiring a fixed point. It is for this reason that religious man *[sic]* has always sought to fix his abode at the "center of the world." *If the world is to be lived in,* it must be *founded*—and no world can come to birth in the chaos of the homogeneity and relativity of profane space. The discovery or projection of a fixed point—the center—is equivalent to the creation of the world...[34]

The *center of the world* is the place where the deity(ies) created everything, and therefore the place that has access to everywhere. Selecting landmarks in the North, South, East, and West from the center helps to define reality, the territory that is known to your tribe. Sacred mountains, World Trees, Jacob's Ladder, shamanic poles, the column of smoke rising from a sacred fire, etc., all mark such a world-originating point, and include the idea of a symbolic way to reach the other worlds. When you declare the presence of a ritual center in your ceremony, you are reinforcing the concept of sacred time (by harking back to when the world was created at this spot), as well as stating that you now have the ability to communicate with other worlds. This combination is very powerful.

It really doesn't matter that thousands or millions of other places are also being declared to be the center of the world at any given time. As Eliade puts it:

> The multiplicity, or even the infinity, of centers of the world raises no difficulty for religious thought. For it is not a matter of geometrical space, but of an existential and sacred space that has an entirely different [quantum?] structure, that admits of an infinite number of breaks and hence is capable of an infinite number of communications with the transcendent.[35]

The creation of a ritual center is often symbolized in Paleo-, Meso-, and Neopagan ceremonies as opening the Gates Between the Worlds. This is usually accomplished by calling upon a particular spirit who is a gatekeeper, and who is easy to contact, since he/she is usually halfway into this world already. The gatekeeper is then asked to open the gates, which she/he usually does with little fuss.

When the gates are opened, exactly where are they? With a round ritual area, they usually seem to manifest in the center and anywhere from three to ten feet above the floor or ground. With rectangular ritual areas, the gates seem to open over the altar or other focus of attention (near the cross or crucifix in a Catholic mass, for example). Obviously, different groups working with different liturgies will visualize and perceive their sacred centers differently (if at all), and this is something that should be discussed during your planning sessions and a consensus decided upon.

In Wiccan rituals, the conscious ritual center is most often just over the altar or the center of the circle (when the altar is off-center). However, an argument can be made that the *entire* sacred space (the cast circle) is a ritual center (between the worlds) and that the spirits invoked at the four directions are all gatekeepers.[36] This all-center technique may only work with sacred spaces that are physically small (such as the classic nine-foot diameter Wiccan circle).

One way to demonstrate and reinforce the location of the ritual center, and to focus thoughts towards invoking the gatekeeper(s), is to choreograph movement around the center's intended location during the center's creation/recognition.

When you become aware of the ritual center you establish a relationship between the people in the sacred space and persons/places/things outside of it. If you're not going to be bringing in mana from the outside (by invoking spirits or deities, for example), then you can skip this step, as well as all of phases three and four. However, you're then no longer doing a worship ceremony, but rather some sort of pure magical or psychic working. Even under those circumstances, if you are attempting to affect something at a distance, you may still want to have a ritual center available through which to send your mana at a distant target.‡

One metaphor for this whole process of defining a ritual center, or opening the gates, is that you are tuning the group mind's psychic awareness to whatever wavelength the ancestors, spirits, and/or gods will be communicating on. Another is that you are taking advantage of the multiverse's quantum entanglement (see *RE*), in which every particle can be viewed as the center of everything and connected to every other one. It doesn't really matter whether you think that you are creating the sacred center or merely recognizing or *manifesting* one that was already there. Whatever explanation you choose, the use of these powerful archetypal concepts is irreplaceable.

Preliminary Power Raising

Now that the gates are open, it's time to start getting everyone's psychic juices flowing (although some folks who are familiar with the ritual may have started generating mana when the ceremony began). This preliminary power raising may be done by singing or chanting, by a sacred dance, or by formal evocations or invocations. All of

‡ See Chapter 9, Cones of Power and Working Through the Center.

these techniques should be focused on the spiritual entities (such as nature spirits, ancestors, or deities) who are associated with the various *worlds* in the cosmos you are re-creating, thus giving both an intellectual and an emotional shape to your group's mental images. The important thing is to get mana to start flowing in and around the ritual area, and to open the participants to this flow.

Phase Three: The Major Gifting of Mana

Descriptive Invocation of the Deity(ies) of the Occasion

This has two primary purposes: to invoke the attention of the god(s) and/or goddess(es) who are the focus of the rite, and to describe him/her/them to the worshippers clearly enough to enable everyone to get a psychic fix onto whom they will send their energy. This descriptive invocation can take the form of a simple prayer, a song, a chant, a litany, a poem, a prose description, a dance, or a story. The richer the multisensory images, the more effective this will be.

Primary Power Raising

Now is the point in the liturgy where the participants will generate as much mana as they can, in order to give it to the one(s) they are worshipping. Remember that this can be accomplished through almost any activity that is capable of getting the participants excited. In Neopagan ceremonies the commonest techniques are to use songs, chants, drumming, poetry, music, dance, and ritual drama.[§] Some liturgies stress building up the mana to a peak, others the creation of multiple waves of power.[¶] Either way, this step will blend into and/or culminate with the sacrifice.

The Sacrifice

The Sacrifice is the point at which the mana raised is symbolically (and therefore magically and spiritually) gathered, focused, and sent

---

§ See Chapter 9, Raising and Focusing Mana.

¶ See Chapter 9, Masculine vs. Feminine Spell/Prayer Casting.

as a gift through the gates to the deity(ies) of the occasion. Usually special prayers, chants, and gestures are used to ensure that all present coordinate their actions. While there may have been lesser sacrifices or offerings to the spirits earlier in the preliminary power raising step, this is the major one for the liturgy.**

Phase Four: Receiving and Using the Returned Power

Preparation for the Return

The return flow of spiritual power is what the whole process of a worship ritual leads up to, so it's important that everyone be ready to receive and handle the divine mana that is to be returned through the gates. Making them ready is usually done through, first, a meditation upon personal and group needs, and second, the induction of a state of receptivity.

The first task is relatively simple: the presiding clergyperson asks everyone present to meditate upon what they, as individuals and/or as a group, need from the deity(ies) of the occasion. In a primarily theurgical ceremony, receiving individual blessings will *be* the main point (the goal) of the entire liturgy. So, folks should be given half a minute or so to think quietly, with no sounds other than those provided by Nature, or perhaps some serene music. Next the participants are reminded of the group's magical/religious goal(s) and target(s) and of the need for unity to achieve them.††**

The second task is a matter of getting the participants into a state of maximum openness and receptivity by reminding them of what is about to happen and why. A prayer, chant, or guided meditation can be used to encourage people to drop whatever remaining psychic shields or emotional blocks they may have between themselves and the deities.

** See Chapter 9, Sacrifices.
†† See Chapter 9, Targets and Goals.

Groups that are musically inclined, for example, could write a quiet, powerful song to accomplish all these tasks, with optional verses to guide the pacing and focus. This would probably work best in a verse-plus-chorus or litany format being led by one or two singers, and including long pauses for meditation.

Part of the induction of receptivity in Neopagan Druid rites[37] is the taking of an omen, via ogham sticks, runes, or scrying (etc.), to determine the nature of the blessings that the deity(ies) intend(s) to bestow. The results of this divination then get worked into the meditations.

It should be noted that in Wiccan ceremonies, the induction of receptivity has an additional aspect, in that the presiding priestess usually intends to *draw down the moon* upon herself. This means that she intends to become possessed by, channel, or at least be inspired by, the Goddess being worshipped.‡‡ This generally requires that she go into a preparatory trance state, usually with the assistance of the priest/ess with whom she is working. Like the other participants, she needs to be placed into a state of maximum openness and receptivity at this point in the ritual, though her trance should be far deeper than that of any other participant.

Reception of Power from the Deity(ies) of the Occasion

There are many ways in which the blessings of the one(s) being worshipped may be received in a ceremony. In a Wiccan rite, the priestess may be inspired or possessed by the Goddess to give information of value to the congregation, along with mana in the form of blessings or healings. The presiding clergy in other rites may make sacred gestures towards each participant, sending the energy coming through the gate(s) to them. All may dance or sing an affirmation that they are receiving the energy, pulling the mana into themselves from the gate(s). The clergy may mark each person's body with a sacred sign

---

‡‡ See *BEGWW* and Chapter 9, Lend Your Aid Unto the Spell: Channeling Energy.

in oil or ashes or some other substance, triggering a transferral of the divine power into the recipients.

By far the most common method is the sharing of drink and/or food that has been blessed/charged with divine power. When a clergyperson consecrates a cup of liquid or a piece of food, she or he is using her/his magical arts to focus and direct the divine power, in order to psychically charge the food or drink, so that each person consuming it opens her/himself to the power of the deity/deities. This process can be invocatory and/or evocatory, depending upon the clergyperson's perceptions of the experience. The energy might seem to be flowing through him/her into the object being consecrated, or it could seem to be coming directly from the ritual center to the object. Either way, this is obviously something that the deity(ies) involved would approve, so he/she/it/they would assist with the charging. In fact, this is exactly what the clergyperson requests during the consecration prayer.

As each person consumes the drink and/or food, he or she physically takes into themselves a substance that has been charged with the energies of the one(s) being worshipped. The symbolic effect of this is extremely powerful. If you believe that you are eating and drinking the energies—or even the flesh and blood—of your deity(ies), this ritual cannibalism (as anthropologists and psychologists call it) will convince your subconscious mind that you are going to become more like her/him/it/them than you were before.

The consumers of consecrated food and drink become psychically, magically, and spiritually wide open to the divine, in the sort of simultaneous surrender/merging/triumph that occurs in the finest lovemaking (which might also explain some of the erotic imagery in the meditations of many mystics). Thus they attain a state, however fleeting, of *communion* (mutual participation or sharing) with the divine.

Since Neopagans believe that divinity is immanent as well as transcendent, this communion can be thought of as a recognition of a state of being that always exists, but which is difficult for most mortals to remember on a day-to-day basis. That recognition can be powerful enough to enable a person to suddenly have access to resources, human and divine, that she or he may have forgotten were available.

Many Wiccan traditions use the blessing of food and drink, and its subsequent consumption, as a grounding technique, since eating and drinking, especially in a social atmosphere, are good ways to bring people back into their bodies after an intense ritual.[38]

Acceptance of Individual Blessings

It is now necessary to accept this divine energy (for any gift may be rejected) and to absorb it into your being for whatever purposes were either originally intended or which the flash of divine fire makes clear at the moment. A chant or song is the most common ritual tool here, or a guided meditation may be done, or a simple statement may be made that "We accept the gift of the Gods and recognize its purpose in our lives."

The emphasis in such a chant, song, or statement should be upon the complete acceptance of this gift of the deity(ies). Mention can be made that the incoming mana will go to where it may be needed most within each person. All who receive the mana should let it fill their bodies and feel it swirling throughout their beings: cleansing, healing, teaching. Whether the ceremony's goals are theurgic or thaumaturgical, at this time individuals should concentrate on their personal relationships with the divine.

The main result of the reception and acceptance of the divine mana is that each participant becomes spiritually and physically exalted. When the return of mana from the deity(ies) is strong, most of the participants will feel themselves filled with mana. If the liturgy has been a spectacular success, some people may cry at this point in the ritual, some may laugh, some may speak in tongues or prophesy. Some may be healed of physical or emotional diseases, while others may receive insights of personal value. Some may receive more mana than they can handle and need help to ground the excess. If a genuine possession should occur (an extremely rare event) the presiding clergy will need to determine and verify the identity of the deity possessing the woman or man, and to inquire after her or his wishes. This may completely change the rest of the ceremony.

After a short pause to digest the mana received and to experience the results—perhaps guided by soft music or a mantra—the ceremony can continue.

Reinforcement of Group Bonding

The next step can have either or both of two intentions: to strengthen the group's awareness of themselves as linked into a group mind at that moment, and/or to make those psychic links continue to connect them to each other long after the ritual is over. This perpetuation of the experience of *communitas* is essential for creating a real community of believers. Once again, this can be accomplished by all participants joining in a chant, song, dance, or by some other activity that would emphasize mutual connections.

If the ritual is purely theurgical, then this step can be a relaxed, schmoozy sort of family awareness, something that can grow through the years. If thaumaturgical work is to be done, this step becomes more important, and the reinforcement of the physical, emotional, intellectual, and spiritual bonds among the participants will need to be clear and unmistakable—you want as much unity in your group mind as you can create before you attempt to cast any sort of spell or prayer. A rite of passage would need both approaches, since most such rituals involve a mixture of thaumaturgy and theurgy.

Optional Activity: Spell Casting or Rite of Passage

Now is when the participants will be able to perform the most powerful spell castings and/or rites of passage, although followers of monotheistic religions will insist what they do at this point is praying rather than spell casting. Of course, since they have now achieved communion with their deity, they expect him to be able to hear their prayers much more clearly (though such is, by their standards, a theologically unsound proposition), and to be more inclined to grant them. Presumably this is because he can now see how sincere and devoted his worshippers are.[§§] Nonetheless, the techniques used in monotheistic ceremonies to get everyone thinking about their desired goals (whether thaumaturgical or theurgical), and to emotionally discharge their energies towards those goals, are separated from polytheistic techniques less by genuine metaphysical or philosophical differences than by levels of effectiveness.

It is possible, of course, that a group of Neopagans, having attained a state of communion with one or more deities, might ask her/him/them to grant a prayer, especially in a situation where a problem appears to go beyond the spell-casting abilities of the group, or where the appropriate goal and target are unknown. However, most Neopagans believe that the gods gave us our magical skills with the intent that we *use* them to manifest their will and ours on the Earth plane level of reality (in this physical world).

So the deities may be asked to send additional power through the participants, or to help with the fine details of visualization and energy direction, but the primary responsibility for the success or failure of the spell rests with the humans involved. If a magical/spiritual/psychic working fails, whether it was thaumaturgical or theurgical, we do not automatically have the excuse available that it was the will of the gods. It might have been their will, but it might also have been incompetence on our part!

Fortunately, if the basic laws of magic[39] and the principles of liturgical design are faithfully observed, the relevant variables are taken into consideration, and the clergy and congregation are competent as well as sincere, most spell castings/prayers and rites of passage done at this point of the ceremony should succeed.

PHASE FIVE: ENDING THE CEREMONY

It's common for the endings of most rituals to mirror, in briefer form, their beginnings. Perhaps this brevity is because it is always easier

---

§§ Why it should be necessary to demonstrate anything, even sincerity, to an omniscient deity is unclear.

to destroy a pattern than to create it (the basic principle of entropy). Yet because of the levels of power involved, it's safest to unwind the patterns of mana carefully and respectfully. In the Vedic rituals of ancient India, for example, according to Brian K. Smith,

> The introductory and concluding rites are likened to the two sides of the chariot and should be symmetrical: "He who makes them equal to one another safely reaches the world of heaven, just as one takes any desired journey by driving a chariot with two sides."[40]

Each step in this phase of the ritual quickly but methodically reverses the steps that grew the liturgy during the first four phases. Parts of the symbolism may also reverse, for example, dancing anticlockwise to unwind mana patterns created by earlier clockwise dancing. Whatever the techniques used, the final result should be an emotionally and aesthetically satisfying sense of closure.

Thanking of Entities Invoked/Invited

This portion of the ceremony accomplishes two tasks: (a) it shows courtesy to the entities invoked and invited, and (b) it lets the Deity(ies) and the lesser entities, not to mention the people, know that you are winding things down and that they can leave if they wish.

Remember the phrase, "Last in, first out." Farewells are said to the spirits invoked or invited in the reverse of the order by which they arrived. The special divine Guest(s) is/are thanked first, because they are usually the last to appear in the liturgy.

You do not dismiss *goddesses and gods.* If nothing else, it's rude. True, some ancient Egyptian magicians were supposedly in the habit of bossing their deities around, as were the purported witches in Charles Leland's *Aradia,* and some modern users of Hoodoo. However, I've always considered these to be corruptions of the earlier states of these religions, something that happens when the magicians involved no longer believe in their deities *as deities.*

In the fully-developed Afro-American Mesopagan religions, the initiated clergy will sometimes have to urge a possessing deity to leave her/his "horse" (the human being possessed). However, I believe that they do this through reminding the deity of the contractual agreements made at the time of the clergyperson's initiation. It's done with love, courtesy, and respect—not with the typical arrogance of the medieval ceremonial magician (the source of Wiccan-style dismissals).

After the deities, you may say farewell to ancestors, nature spirits, angels, etc., maintaining the reverse order. Eventually this leads to the following.

Thanking the Gatekeeper and Closing the Gates

Having been the first to be formally invited to the ritual, the gatekeeper is the last to be thanked. The Gates Between the Worlds that he/she opened need to be *closed*. Granted, they will eventually close on their own, after a few hours or days, but in the meantime the lives of the participants may be visited by a wide variety of energies from the Other Side, not all of them pleasant. So it's a good idea to formally ask the gatekeeper to close them as she/he leaves. If any sort of physical activity (such as a dance, or particular gestures) was done to open the gates, a similar activity (symbolically reversed) should be done to close them again. In a Wiccan rite, this step in the ritual would involve the spirits of the four quarters.

Affirmations of Continuity and Success

Near the beginning of the ritual you pointed out the historical precedents for what you intended to do (the ceremony and any specific thaumaturgical or theurgical workings). Now, in the process of reversing the ritual, you reiterate that what you have done is traditional in some fashion or another, that the deities and the ancestors have been pleased, and that the participants are part of an historic whole stretching into the past and future. Even if your group has only existed a few decades, years, or weeks, you can still refer to ancient habits of thought and behavior that you have imitated, to ancient spirits whom you have worshipped, and/or to ancient customs that you have revived.

It is useful here to also state that others will be doing rituals similar to yours in the future, that those present are part of a continuous line reaching from the distant past to the distant future. This *affirmation of continuity* will give the participants the necessary sense of connection with the human past, making it easier in the future for them to contact those ancient energies, mortal and immortal. It also provides a sense of validation by strengthening their beliefs that what they are doing is important and will last.

Having told everyone's subconscious mind that the ceremony was properly done from a traditional point of view, and that others will do similar rites in the future, you also need to tell them that it worked in present time as well, that the ritual purpose specified early in the ceremony was indeed accomplished.

Those of you who are familiar with golf, tennis, bowling, baseball, croquet, or any other sport that involves casting or striking a small object away from you, will know about the importance of *follow-through*. You don't just stop moving abruptly the instant the ball is struck or thrown, you continue the bodily motions you were engaged in at that instant. This makes sure that your motions will be smooth and continuous, rather than abrupt and jerky, and thus improves the accuracy of your casting/striking.

This metaphor works well for casting spells instead of objects. This is true even for purely theurgical workings in which you are, in essence, casting a spell upon yourself, and thus for worship ceremonies in which you have received a spell cast upon you by the deity(ies). The way you follow through in a ritual is by proclaiming that the blessings have been received, the spell is already working, etc. This *affirmation of success* alerts your subconscious to stop receiving and/or sending mana. Just as importantly, it tells your subconscious to let go of the target(s) psychically. Without this letting go, your subconscious is likely to continue worrying at the target(s) long after the ritual is over, which usually has the effect of draining away the mana sent, often ruining the results. So you need to have your conscious mind say to your subconscious mind (and any spirits who might be listening), "Hey! It worked!"

The affirmations of continuity and success can also be seen as the culmination of a pattern of announcing, doing, and reporting that describes most of the ceremony in process, as well as many successful speeches, dramas, and other forms of storytelling.

Unmerging, Unlinking, Regrounding, and Recentering

Now it's necessary to bring people back in touch with their normal state of consciousness, regardless of whether you have done a spell casting, a rite of passage, or neither. Otherwise folks will drift in their altered states indefinitely, and the mana absorbed and/or channeled will not be properly "digested." At this point the presiding clergy should remind the participants to refocus their attention by thinking about what they've been doing, feeling the emotions that have been generated as a result, and sensing their physical connections to the realm of mortals again. This recovery process will continue through the rest of the ceremony, gradually returning everyone to ordinary states of being (though we hope in an improved condition).

In keeping with the unwinding process, it's now necessary to go through these steps: to unmerge the group mind, to disconnect the psychic links (though some will remain *in potentia*), to return the participants to a more mundane consciousness, and to recenter them within themselves as unique individuals. This is usually done through a guided meditation of some sort, which should use phrases and internal patterns similar to the ones used at the beginning of the ceremony when the group mind was created.

Draining Off Excess Mana

It often occurs that one or more participants may have been overloaded with energy during the ceremony, and may have more left at this point than they can handle. Now is the time to drain off that excess mana. This can be done as a part of the regrounding meditation just described, and/or in conjunction with a special act done with some clear symbolism, such as pouring out any remaining sacred fluids upon the earth.

The excess mana, from the participants and/or the leftover consecrated liquids, is drained away into the ground beneath the participants. This is not a *libation*, although it sometimes is called that, since technically libations are sacred offerings of food and/or drink, given to the Gods or other spirits as part of a religious or mundane meal, or as a sacrifice within a liturgy (a literal feeding of the deities). The excess mana should be given to the Earth with the intent that the immediate physical area be healed of any harm that has been done to its ecosystem. With indoor rites, the liquids should be saved and taken outside immediately afterward. In effect, this is one last spell being cast by the participants, and all the usual laws of magic apply. That's why the energy is focused locally and not given to the Earth as a whole—the latter would be too vague a target for effective magic. As time goes by, people using the same site for their liturgies will notice that it's greener and healthier than when they began.

Some people, however, prefer to drain off any excess mana into their ceremonial tools, thus strengthening them for future use.

Deconsecration of Space

Your ritual space will need to be deconsecrated, unless you are lucky enough to have a temple building or sacred grove that you are confident will remain holy. Deconsecration of temporary space is necessary to prevent outsiders from wandering through a charged area and accidentally connecting up with the psychic links of the folks who have been worshipping there. More importantly, it is necessary to announce to the subconscious minds of the participants that they are back in the real world of day-to-day life again.

This can be done by symbolically opening a door or gate to the outside world, cutting across the line of a cast circle with a sword, saying "Let us go forth into the world," or by other symbolic ways of reconnecting to mundane space. This step is often combined with the next.

Clear-Cut Ending: Deconsecration of Time

Just as each ritual needs a clear-cut beginning, it also needs an equally definite ending—an overt cue to each person's subconscious that it's no longer magic time. So announce that "this ceremony is over" verbally, then follow up with snuffing out the candles, ringing a bell, having a recessional away from the site, or playing a special piece of music.

If you started the ritual with a specific sound, such as a bell ringing or a horn blast, this same sound should be the last one of the liturgy. This brings the ceremony full circle.

After the Rite

You are not finished just because the ceremony is over! The clergy and other organizers still have things they will need to do afterward.¶¶

When the occasion is appropriate, you should follow a successful ritual with a party, or at least some celebratory food and drink. It's true that the prospect of coffee hour afterward is what often brings folks to attend ceremonies week after week, but I have something more in mind here. Strong, well-performed liturgies will satisfy the conscious and superconscious minds of the participants, but their subconscious minds will prefer their rewards a bit earthier. Your inner child usually appreciates a chance to relax and have fun with old and new friends. Eating and drinking also help folks to ground out any excess mana not gotten rid of previously.

Now that we have a clear idea of the abstract structure of an effective liturgy, let's take a look at the first of many practical factors that will decide how well your liturgical design can be executed.

¶¶ See Chapter 12, Post-Ritual Cleanup and Critiques.

4

People Factors in Liturgical Design

Liturgical Variables

A *variable* is, quite simply, something that *varies* or changes from situation to situation. In mathematics and other sciences, the word is used for factors in equations where the amounts of mass or force or speed or gravity or whatever may change from one case to another. Most of the calculations done by clergy and other magical workers are *qualitative* ones rather than quantitative ones, and are done intuitively rather than rationally. Still, the concept of variables is appropriate, since when mana is being used we are faced with a need to handle dozens (or hundreds or thousands) of unknown factors, many of which are in a constant state of change.

The reason why even the greatest priests, priestesses, shamans, and magicians in the real world fail so frequently (especially with thaumaturgically-focused rituals), is that there are just too many variables to keep track of at the same time—many of which may be beyond the ability of any mortal to identify or control. When you have deities or other spirits assisting, as in most rituals that are predominantly theurgical, you have them to keep track of some of those extra variables—which is another reason why they are so often invoked in most rituals of all sorts.

The complexity of magical and religious phenomena is certainly on a level with that of quantum physics, biochemistry, or cosmology. Still, there are certain major variables that have been isolated over the centuries by magical and religious workers. Juggling these correctly will contribute to your ritual success.

In this chapter, let's begin with what may be the most important factors for liturgical designers: the people (and spirits) who will be participating in your ritual.

ORGANIZATIONAL STRUCTURE, LEADERSHIP, AND AGENDAS

These three interwoven factors constitute the soil in which your decisions about the other factors will sprout or wither, because they deal with the fundamental process of decision-making in a liturgical context. You and the members of your group need to decide who will be making what decisions, with how much authority, based on what your group's obvious and hidden purposes are, before any other decisions—including liturgical ones—can be made.

Organizational Structure

Every intentional group of people—a softball team, a sewing circle, a dental office, a coven of Witches, or a grove of Druids—has some sort of organizational structure, obvious or invisible, to regulate and guide their power relationships. For many Neopagans, Starhawk[41] has most clearly articulated what they consider an appropriate philosophy of different types of power, and the institutions and organizations that support them: power that is exercised *over* other people is evil, power that is exercised *with* others is good, and power that comes from *within* each person is best. Her writings, which have been widely influential in the Neopagan, feminist, and women's spirituality movements, show a clear bias against hierarchy and in favor of egalitarianism. Yet what do these terms really mean?

Hierarchy originally referred to sacred rule in ancient Egypt—a situation where the clergy made major social, political, economic, and (of course) religious decisions for their tribes. Today it usually means any religious, political, social, and/or economic system where power is exercised by a minority, organized into levels of rank, with a few people near the top making the most important decisions. Examples would include many churches, most business corporations, most surgical teams, most theatrical production companies, any army or navy, etc. The theory behind hierarchy is that the individuals with the most knowledge and experience should have the most power (and need it in order to function effectively). In practice, as we all know, people in power are often reluctant to retire (even when better-qualified replacements are available), frequently object to sharing even a small portion of their power and prestige, did not necessarily get into power through honest means, and are, in any event, fallible mortals. Plus, there is the "Peter Principle"—that people rise in hierarchies until they reach their level of incompetence, at which point they stop getting promoted but can still cause damage to the organization. Unfortunately, this works in religious organizations as easily as it does in secular ones.[42]

Egalitarianism (equal-ism) was not a particularly positive word until the French Revolution. The theory, based intellectually on Luther's idea of the "priesthood of all believers" (see below) and emotionally on the revolt against the corrupt French nobility, was that nobody was better than anybody else in matters that really counted. Everybody had a soul and a nobleman's wasn't any more valuable than that of a peasant (as long as they were both white, male, and Christian). Eventually the egalitarian theory expanded to include most human beings, and birthed the idea that people of good will could sit down together and pool their knowledge to make wise decisions. In practice, the idea that everyone in a group is equally qualified to make complex decisions has often led to disaster.

How do these ideas apply to liturgy? In some groups, the decisions about ceremonial matters are made by the person(s) believed (correctly or not) to be most knowledgeable about ritual— these people usually get called "clergy." In other groups, all members discuss the issues and vote their preferences, blithely assuming the majority opinion will be the correct one. In still others, conversation continues until a consensus has been reached (meaning until every single person says that he or she agrees with the others). Groups of this last sort may not have people called clergy at all, nor recognize any special knowledge or skill that entitles anyone's opinions to be considered more important than those of the others in the group (although covert leadership almost always develops).

Each of these approaches to decision-making has strengths and weaknesses. Trained clergy usually *do* know enough about liturgy to supervise its creation and performance quickly and effectively; democratic majorities can at least balance out the desires of a congregation with the opinions of clergy; consensus opinion-forming does insure that no one feels left out of the decision-making process and that everyone feels empowered by having her/his opinion valued. Yet, as we all know, elites can easily become tyrannical, democratic majorities are frequently wrong about matters of fact and art, and the consensus process usually results in rule by the lowest common denominator (not to mention taking forever to achieve).

In each case, the quality of the decision-making depends upon the quality of the people: are they intelligent, educated, knowledgeable about ritual, and sensitive to the psychological nuances of group interaction? If so, almost any of these approaches will work. But if the people are not all such paragons, they may be in for trouble.

Groups that are hierarchical tend to emphasize results over process—as long as the ceremony, for example, turns out well (however the group defines that), the fact that some members got their feelings hurt is considered trivial. Consensus groups usually emphasize process over results—one consensus tradition of Wicca proudly claims, "Process is our most important product!"—but they may not care or even notice if the ritual turns out poorly.

My personal, professional biases are toward a combination of the hierarchical and consensus approaches. I believe that every religious group should have a temporary or permanent ritual leader, who should be acknowledged as such, and who should be trained in and competent at designing, preparing, and performing liturgies. She/he should spend enough time talking to the rest of the group to enable her/him to have a clear idea of the others' wants and needs, and should pay attention to the group dynamics involved. Then she/he should be allowed to make the relevant decisions, alone or with assistants, until such a time as the group decides that she/he is no longer producing powerful, effective, and satisfying liturgies of the sort that the group desires. Then a new ritual leader should be chosen, preferably by consensus—otherwise the new leader will have trouble getting everyone to cooperate psychically during ceremonies.

The ritual leader of a group does not have to be the philosophical, political, or emotional leader of a group, but she/he does need to have the members of the group trust her/him. Just as brilliant works of art are seldom created by committee, so too, magnificent liturgies are rarely the product of second guessing your chief liturgist. This leads us to the whole topic of leadership in general and the necessity or irrelevance of clergy.

Leadership

Does your group have temporary, long-term, or permanent leaders at all? If so, how were they chosen? What were their qualifications? What roles, such as clergy, bards,[43] therapists, polytheologians, or choreographers, do they play? Are these roles predetermined by training and experience, or do they rotate among the members of the group?

Throughout this book I use *clergy* as a short term for the people most likely to be leading the creation, preparation, and performance of liturgies. I believe the role of clergy to be an important one and that their leadership, if based on genuine competence, is a good idea. Within the Neopagan community, however, and throughout the entire spectrum of liberal religions, the whole question of clergy is a hot one.

Among the Indo-European Paleopagans most cultures believed that anyone could contact the gods and goddesses or do simple folk magic, but that certain sorts of religious activities, especially those that involved large numbers of people or particularly difficult magic, required the presence of specialists (the druids, flamens, or brahmans). During the rise of Christianity, the general population was discouraged from doing any sort of religious activities, other than private prayer and meditation, without the direction of a priest. This eventually led to Martin Luther's rebellion and his formulation of the doctrine Christian theologians call "the priesthood of all believers." As Van A. Harvey explains:

> Luther thought of it as a correlate of the doctrines of justification by faith alone and of the liberty of the Christian believer. Like other Protestant affirmations, this one has a positive and a negative meaning. Positively, it means that just as every Christian has an inner liberty of conscience that makes him a "lord over all," so, too, every Christian is a priest or "servant of all." By this Luther meant not simply that every man has his own direct access to Christ but that all Christians are "worthy to appear before God to pray for others and to teach one another the things of God." Negatively, this means not only a rejection of the medieval tradition that practically identified priesthood with the administration of the sacraments but also constitutes an attack on the conception of priesthood as constituting a special class in the eyes of God with a special power and a higher morality. Luther insisted that the public ministry was simply a matter of practical function or vocation. It followed that it was not a higher or more religious form of life with a special standing in God's eyes. The Anabaptists, that other part of the Reformation too frequently forgotten, took the phrase to mean the complete abolishment of any functional distinction between clergy and laity. No believer was believed to have any status or function not fully shared by all.[44]

These concepts have influenced Western culture for the last four hundred years, affecting both liberal and conservative Protestants. In the 1930s–1950s, when Gerald Gardner was creating Wicca (which was to become Neopagan Witchcraft), he was still Mesopagan enough that he took this Protestant Christian doctrine and enshrined it into Wiccan duotheology and liturgy. In Gardner's case, the concept became what we could call "the clergyhood of all believers," and every

Wiccan was named "Priestess and Witch" or "Priest and Witch" upon their first initiation into the faith.

Members of modern liberal religions with scientistic biases against magic can be forgiven for clinging to Luther's doctrines, but Gardner really should have known better. As a practicing ceremonial magician and amateur anthropologist, he was aware that magic is an art and a science that requires both talent and training, and that priest/ess-hood requires (among many other things) skill in magic—making it something that not everyone is going to be equally good at. Yet rather than go back to the earlier Paleopagan attitudes about clergy, he chose to perpetuate the Protestant Christian ones, probably because it fit with his vision of Witchcraft as a peasants' religion.

Even today Neopagan groups tend to be ambivalent about having clergy. Most have some sort of priests and/or priestesses, yet the degree of respect and authority granted to them varies widely. A given group's attitude about leadership in general and clergy in particular is often a product of its attitudes about hierarchy and egalitarianism, as reflected in the internal structure of the group. Those groups with radical political and/or feminist agendas (see below) often refuse to label anyone as clergy, having completely accepted the patriarchal Anabaptist doctrine Van Harvey describes about the nondistinction between clergy and laity.

Agendas

Once you think you've settled the issues of leadership and group structure, you've got to make explicit all of your agendas—both overt and covert, individual and group. First, because those agendas may force you to modify your decisions about leadership and structure. Second, because your agendas will determine just how important good liturgy really is to your group.

Overt agendas are the official reasons why your group has gotten together, and these can be spiritual, political, ecological, social-interpersonal, artistic, therapeutic/theurgic, thaumaturgical, healing, and/or recreational. *Covert agendas* are usually individual motivations that you may not want the general public, or even your fellow group members, to know about. They usually involve psychologically dysfunctional motives, such as an urge to be the constant center of attention, a need to rebel against authority figures, a desire to curse your enemies, wanting to fix all the world's ills, or an addiction to ritual energies.

If your group's overt agenda is a radical political one, for example, you may well decide to do without hierarchy and have only temporary leaders, if any, regardless of the impact this may have on the quality of your ceremonies. If it's artistic, you may decide to have the best artist in the group be the leader on a fairly permanent basis, and give her/him strong authority to run the show. A group that is mostly interested in creating a schmoozy family feeling, or in having a good time, is likely to be less worried about excellence in liturgy than a group whose primary agenda is to heal physical and emotional ailments.

Covert agendas are likely to have negative effects unless they are brought out and discussed in the group. If your group has an overt agenda that requires a strong leader and lots of hierarchy, while several of the members have covert agendas to resist authority figures and structures, or vice versa, you're in trouble. You're not only setting yourself up for a difficult time doing satisfying liturgy, you're setting the stage for an eventual blowup of the group.[45]

Assumptions for the Rest of the Book

As far as the issues of leadership and structure are concerned, I'll assume that you have decided to have clergy in your group, as well as specialists performing various roles, such as musicians, diviners, healers, or choreographers. Further, I'll assume that these people were chosen— permanently or temporarily—on the basis of genuine knowledge and competence; and that they have enough authority within a hierarchy of some sort that the other members of the group (and any guests at your liturgies) will follow their lead most of the time. I'll even assume that the members of your group have no overt or covert agendas that will interfere with making the best possible liturgical decisions to fulfill their needs, however much those agendas may have affected other issues.

I know what happens when one assumes— especially assumptions as optimistic as these! Nonetheless, I'm going to proceed this way because these conditions are the ones that I have seen associated with the most powerful, beautiful, and effective liturgies I have witnessed or led. As a liturgist and writer, I want to teach people how to accomplish such powerful, beautiful, and effective liturgies. You are, of course, expected to modify my advice based on the actual situation in your group and the resources available to you.

†HE ΠUMBER OF PEOPLE ÍNVOLVED

The most often overlooked factor, major or minor, in liturgy is the number of people who will be present. To begin with, the following rough size categories may prove useful for our purposes:

Number	Term
1:	Solitary Ritual
2:	Dyadic or Couple Ritual
3–7:	Very Small Group Ritual
7–15:	Small Group Ritual
15–40:	Medium Group Ritual
40–100:	Large Group Ritual
100–200	Very Large Group Ritual
200–500:	Small Crowd Ritual
500–1000:	Medium Crowd Ritual
1000–5000:	Large Crowd Ritual
5000+:	Very Large Crowd Ritual

Obviously, it's possible to have rituals with many thousands of people involved, so the single term "very large crowd" may be inadequate for exploring the distinctions between a ceremony with, for example, 7,500 participants and one with 750,000. Although Neopagan worship ceremonies, as such, may not have that many people in them for a few decades to come, Neopagan rituals at large gatherings of overlapping subcultures (such as the Rainbow Festivals, feminist conventions, ecology marches, anti-nuclear demonstrations, etc.) have already involved thousands in the past and may easily attract tens of thousands in the near future. No doubt new vocabulary will be created as needed.

During the last forty-five years, the Neopagan community has done a great deal of experimentation with solitary, dyadic, very small, and small group ritual techniques, but has had problems with larger populations. Most Neopagans have simply assumed that the small group methods invented by Gerald Gardner and his friends when they were creating Wicca would work for larger groups or crowds. This has proven false. Let me give this the appropriate amount of stress:

> *You cannot simply take the techniques that work well with seven people in your living room and use them with four hundred people at a festival.*

Putting it as optimistically as possible, I can say that each increase in the size of your congregation brings forth new challenges and new opportunities for the aspiring liturgist.

During my career, I have led or otherwise participated in magical and religious rituals of every size mentioned except the very large crowd. Despite the difficulties, I continue to be enthusiastic about the larger ones because as the number of people increases arithmetically, the amount of mana that is (at least potentially) available for magical and/or spiritual use increases *geometrically*. Considering how much work needs to be done to save the Earth Mother, I think we need all the magical and spiritual energy we can get.

Intra-Group Familiarity

Interwoven with the question of sheer size is that of how familiar the participants are with each other. This factor is crucial to the successful creation of a group mind, as discussed previously.[*] That creation is one of the major steps of any liturgy or other group artistic endeavor.

---

[*] See Chapter 3, Phase One.

The intra-group familiarity factor breaks down into three subcategories: knowledge, affection, and group identity.

A small group of people who already know each other well can often generate more *usable* mana than a larger group of people who don't. If you know, for example, how well the other members of your group can chant, or drum, or visualize, then you have a better idea of how to blend your energies with theirs to create the group mind. You might decide that you'll need to put the person with the strongest voice next to the one with the weakest, for example, or perhaps change the length of your guided meditations to match the group's collective experience and skill.

If the people in a group have bonds of genuine friendship or love between them, their ability to perform ritual will be greatly enhanced. The psychic and psychological barriers that most people keep between themselves will be fewer and more easily set aside. This is why Wiccans place so much emphasis on "perfect love and perfect trust"—love and trust, even when imperfect, tend to strengthen each other and increase a group's psychological and psychic unity.

Even if a group of people has never met before, they can, all other factors being equal, generate and focus their mana more effectively if they all share some sort of group identity. The more specific this group identity is, the better it will work for this purpose. "We are all Gardnerians" or "we are all Georgians" (two denominations of Neopagan Witchcraft) will work better as a concept than "we are all Witches." Likewise, "We are all Neopagan Druids" or "we are all Reformed Druids" will work better than just plain "we are all Druids." "We are all Unitarian Universalists" will work better than "we are all religious liberals."

These three aspects of intra-group familiarity influence how effective a group mind you're going to be able to create and maintain with the people present. Acquaintanceship creates intellectual and social bonds, while friendship and love create emotional ones. All of these bonds can function as *psychic links* (metaphorical channels through which mana flows), as can, to a lesser extent, the psychological bonds created by group identity. The more psychic links that already exist among the people participating in your liturgy, the easier it will be to create and maintain the group consciousness necessary for a successful ritual. Acknowledging and activating these links is a major function of the recitation of *creeds* (statements of group belief) and other prayers said early in many liturgies.

Throughout this book, I'll be mentioning how the other factors to be discussed are affected by those of population and intra-group familiarity. *Having more people present makes more mana available, yet also makes it harder to keep that mana focused.* A very large part of liturgical design deals with how to create and maintain the group mind at whatever size level is called for.

Familiarity with the Liturgy

If the same people show up for rituals regularly, and the ritual is essentially the same each time (as it probably will be if everyone belongs to the same denomination or tradition), then they will be thoroughly familiar with the liturgy, and your major worry will be boredom. If many of them only show up once in a while, you'll need obvious cues and movement instructions built into the script. This is even more important if many or most of the participants have never been to a liturgy of this type before. If there is a broad range of ritual experience in the expected congregation, your ritual design needs plenty of things for the inexperienced members to do, with built-in instructions on how to do them, yet with the cues not being offensive to the more experienced members.

One solution is to have the majority of your liturgy be the same each time, but have a minority of it change to reflect each occasion. In the Catholic mass, for example, this distinction is that between the "Ordinary" and the "Proper," where the former is the same every time and the latter changes from occasion to occasion. Some Neo-pagan rites accomplish this by invoking different gods and/or goddesses as the primary deity(ies) for a ceremony, and/or by having new chants and songs for different occasions.

You can also vary an occasion by having special visual effects: banners, altar cloths, costumes, etc., in the colors and with the symbols appropriate to the occasion and/or the deity(ies) involved.

Shared Worldview, Mythology, and Poly/theology

A writer named Trip Gabriel, discussing ceremonies he had witnessed in the men's spirituality movement of the 1980s, said:

> It seems to me that there is a problem with the search for latter-day rituals by the men's movement. In themselves, rituals performed outside a cultural context don't mean very much. The power of a rite, be it a Christmas mass or an Indian sweat lodge, comes from what the participants bring to it, which is the result of a long history of beliefs and expectations... Enacted without a pre-existing system of beliefs, the drumming, dancing, and vision questing of the new masculinity feel pretty silly—at least they do to this camper.[46]

He has pointed out a very important factor in the creation of effective liturgies: if the people who are participating in your ritual don't share certain religious and philosophical values, however vaguely perceived or expressed, then a ceremony that seems powerful to some will seem meaningless (or even silly) to others. Fortunately, mens' rituals—at least in the Neopagan movement—have improved considerably since Gabriel wrote those words (see *PM*).

The more your participants know and accept the intellectual, artistic, psychological, social, and spiritual worldviews to be expressed by your liturgy, the more effective they will be at forming a group mind and the more each individual will get out of their experience.

One solution is to have a *pre-ritual briefing*.† Though you won't usually have the time to give a full lecture on the cosmology, mythology, and/or polytheology behind your ritual, you can at least answer

---

† See the section of that title in Chapter 11.

any outstanding questions that a newcomer might have, including about any aspects of your liturgy that might seem to be secular rather than spiritual to some.

If the worldviews expressed by your liturgy include ideas and images that some of the people participating in your liturgy will strongly disagree with, then you should either discuss them at length during the planning process, or at least announce them during the pre-ritual briefing, so that people may choose not to participate. If, for example, you have agnostics or atheists present, you will need to persuade them to consider the spirits to be mentioned to be, at the very least, metaphors or symbols of important concepts.

If you are doing a ceremony that involves heterosexual symbolism (as in most Wiccan rites), or which implies that all magic requires both genders to cooperate (again, as in most Wiccan metaphysical systems), participants who are gay or lesbian, or who belong to gender separatist groups, may be offended and withdraw from the group mind you are attempting to create and maintain.

Alternately, a ceremony in which you invoke ancient African deities and declare how they are superior to all others, will offend pluralists and most non-Africans present. A guided meditation in which you casually state, "All cabbage worshippers are turkey-pluckers!" will offend current and ex-cabbagists (and possibly any real turkey-pluckers who may have joined your group). Some may be shocked by a ritual drama or a chant that mentions an incident of divine incest or zoophilia. It's wisest to sort all this out long before the ceremony begins.

OTHER ASPECTS OF GROUP HOMOGENEITY

Homogeniety, as I'm using it in this book, is a matter of how similar the people in your group are to each other. Similarity or divergence in average age, in gender, in sexual preferences, in ethnic or racial ancestry, in cultural or subcultural preferences, and in their past or present creeds, can all impact your ability to create a shared headspace and the participants' reactions to the images and actions presented in your liturgy. Some of these factors may affect the reactions you receive from deities and other spirits whom you invoke. Heterosexual deities, for example, may be hostile or indifferent to homosexual, bisexual, or transgendered people, or ambisexual deities be annoyed by rigidly straight ones.‡ *Most of these factors do not affect people's basic abilities to do magic or prayer;* yet you still need to be aware of their possible effects on creating the results you desire.

Here's a social and political hot potato for you: are most of your participants going to be of roughly equal intelligence and educational levels? If you discover that most of the people in your congregation aren't very bright, let's say, you will need to use methods that speak to their hearts and their bodies, rather than their intellects.§ If most of them have high IQs and graduate degrees, then you may have a difficult time getting them off their rear ends and generating any mana at all—hence the snooze factor in most High Church Anglican, Unitarian Universalist, Vedanta Society, or Ceremonial Magical rituals.

Connected to the intelligence and education question is that of social class. Some cultures, like those in the United States, like to pretend that they have no classes at all, while others such as the English, the Germans, and the Spanish, have historically been obsessed with the topic. Social snobbery, often combined with racism, can lead a congregation or entire denominations to refuse to use highly powerful and successful methods of generating and focusing spiritual and magical energies, just because "only the lower classes" or "those people" use such "vulgar" music/dance/art in their worship rituals.[47]

Are most of your people introverts (inner-directed) or extroverts (outer-directed)? The former are usually better at the passive psychic and magical arts that involve the reception of energies and information, while the latter are usually better at the active ones that involve sending information and/or mana elsewhere. Introverts usually are more interested in theurgy; extroverts in thaumaturgy. Introverts are often very private about their spiritual life, and prefer Apollonian or

---

‡ Deities, however, are often far more broadminded than their conservative worshippers may wish to acknowledge.

§ Or you might just reevaluate your own membership.

austere art and ritual styles, while extroverts often are very public with their spirituality and lean toward Dionysian, or ecstatic ones. Remember that these three categories of introvert/extrovert, theurgist/thaumaturgist, and Apollonian/Dionysian, represent continuous spectrums between polar opposites. They should be conceived in terms of intersecting coordinate axes or planes, rather than as sets of dualistic opposites that can be simply equated with one another.

Monotheistic theologians emphasized their deity(ies) as completely transcendent, and mortal flesh as evil or at least inferior; so they created liturgical systems that emphasized Apollonian approaches to worship. Ecstatic movements within each of these families of religion, who revived or reinvented the Dionysian means of communicating with the divine, rediscovered the possibility of divine immanence. Naturally, they were denounced as heretics and savagely suppressed by the upholders of orthodoxy (for as long as those upholders had the political, economic, and military power to do so). Even after the founding orthodoxy has lost that secular might, these habits of thought still entwine with upper-class biases (and racism) to affect modern attitudes in many mainstream denominations.

Neopagans, New Agers, and other liberal religionists, not being dualists, are free to dance a middle way between varying degrees of Apollonian intellectual clarity and Dionysian enthusiasm, tailored to the needs of our congregations.

The ease of creating the group mind or communitas can also be affected by the overall physical and mental health of the group. If most of the people have serious illnesses, dysfunctions, or addictions, this will affect how much mana they can generate and how well they can focus their minds and hearts. If everyone is a little bit crazy by mainstream standards, are they crazy in similar or varied fashions?

You will also want to consider the average individual experience level of your group members—not just how many weeks or years of time they have spent practicing magic, art, or religion, but the *quality* of that experience, both in general and with the particular type of liturgy being attempted.⁋ This will connect, via the other factors previously mentioned, to the issue of rigidity or flexibility in their personalities, and thus to their openness to adaptation and change.**

What about patience levels? How long can the rite go on before most of the participants run out of steam? Modern Westerners have pathetically short attention spans compared to our ancestors, in large part due to the influence of mass media and the instant gratification culture it spawned.

This relates to the question of how disciplined most of the members of your group are likely to be. Religious liberals are often afraid of the very concept of religious discipline, and we often confuse the many inner-directed vs. outer-directed forms of discipline available. Unfortunately, self-discipline is directly related to one's ability to keep promises or to truly mean exactly what one says. This is what older generations of occultists referred to as *magical will*, and is crucial to the amount of trust inspired among one's friends and co-religionists. While perfect trust is always an impossible ideal to strive after, moderately good trust—at least about specific topics and activities—is necessary to create sufficient unity for effective group action of any sort, liturgical or secular, including the creation and experience of communitas.

Psychic Skills Available

The actual psychic abilities of the participants in a liturgy constitute an important factor, especially for predominantly thaumaturgical rites, that many people neglect. Paying attention to it does not seem very egalitarian or spiritual to most folks, plus it flies in the face of the (monotheistic) assumptions that the skills of the worshippers are irrelevant to the results of the liturgy.

⁋ As Phaedra puts it, "Have they had ten years of experience or one year ten times?"

** See Chapter 10, Orthodoxy vs. Creativity.

However, if you are doing a ritual to heal someone, and none of the participants happens to be a very good healer, then you are not going to get much in the way of useful results. Unless, that is, you have someone who is good at invoking and/or channeling divine mana and you have her/him contact a god or goddess of healing to provide the necessary fine-tuning of the mana.†† If all of your participants are empathic or precognitive, but none of them has any psychokinetic (mind over matter) talents, then you're going to have trouble getting rituals designed to affect matter to work well, regardless of the sincerity of the participants. *Sincerity is not a substitute for competence.*

Having the right psychic talents available is more of a problem with small groups than with larger ones. The more people you have involved in a ritual, the better chance you have that people with the necessary talents will be present. Since the talents necessary for theurgical results (telepathy, empathy, the clair-senses, etc.) seem to be more widespread than those needed for thaumaturgical results (often the psychokinetic talents), it's usually easier to collect the necessary people for a successful theurgical rite than a thaumaturgical one.[48]

Non-Psychic Skills Available

Almost every single art, and many sciences, can be worked into your liturgies with sufficient thought and imagination. The wise liturgist will find out as much as possible about the creative skills of her/his congregation and will figure out a way for everyone to contribute. Not only does it improve the overall quality of your ceremonies, it greatly increases everyone's sense of participation and belonging.

Nonpsychic talents or skills can sometimes be almost as liturgically important as psychic ones, so people who are psychically head blind (which is sort of like being tone deaf and almost as rare) can still be valuable members of a working congregation.

---

†† See Chapter 9, Lend Your Aid Unto the Spell: Channeling Energy.

Sometimes, finding that a member of your group has an unusual non-psychic talent can lead to new ideas and opportunities for liturgical creativity. Someone mentions that she/he is a weaver—work a weaving motif into a spell casting. A new arrival is a professional violinist—with an hour of rehearsal, you suddenly have accompaniment for songs and chants.‡‡ Someone mentions during a planning session that he/she used to do woodcarving—you may wind up with ceremonial staves or deity statues to use as a focus during your worship.

If you don't have any musicians or singers in your group, it's probably a bad idea to design a liturgy with a heavy musical emphasis unless you can arrange to have a good sound system available for recorded music—but using recorded sounds can have it own problems, as humans aren't always on time or in perfect rhythm. Non-dancers should not be expected to perform complex or strenuous choreography. People afraid of fire should not be appointed fire wardens for an event. If the presiding clergy can't pronounce the Irish, Russian, Latin, or Old Norse prayers that were written, than those prayers should only be done in whatever your group's regular language is.

Don't forget the dramatic possibilities presented by stage magicians and others who have studied theatrical special effects. As long as modern adults participating in your rite *know* that stage magic or special effects are part of the ceremony, there are no ethical issues involved in their use. To pre-scientific peoples, who had different ways of defining reality, any ethical issues here depended upon other ethical factors such as intent and results.

As a liturgical leader, you're not running a parapsychological research laboratory—you're putting on a religious ceremony. Everybody's conscious mind will be aware that trickery is being done, but their subconscious mind will be too busy "oohing" and "aahing" to care.

---

‡‡ But don't *assume* that a professional artist or craftsperson will want to give the fruits of their talents for free.

The Needs and Expectations of All Participants

If some or (Gods forbid!) all of the participants in your liturgy walk away feeling disappointed, bored, or unfulfilled, then your ritual was *not* a success. That means that one or more of the people responsible for the liturgical design, preparation, or performance *failed*. These bitter facts are so unpalatable that most people will say or do almost anything to avoid admitting them. The usual tricks are to simply ignore any negative reactions; to cast aspersions on the folks feeling them (a classic example of the universal human impulse to blame the victim); or to cite supposedly uncontrollable factors such as the weather, astrological events, the will of the Gods, etc. Many liturgical failures, however, could be avoided if people would simply take into account the differing needs and expectations of all the beings whom you expect to participate.

Obviously, if you are going to have fanatic dancers in attendance, they'll expect good dance music and a chance to use it. Goddess worshippers will want you to invoke female deities. Germanophiles will want the ceremony to include German cultural and linguistic elements. New Agers will insist that you insert crystals somewhere, somehow, into your script. All of these examples come under the category of including ideas, arts, symbols, and tools that the members of your group will find exciting. But if you don't know what the members of your group (not to mention any spirits being invited) want and need from your liturgies, you can hardly satisfy them.

Overtly expressed opinions are relatively easy to handle, provided that you keep your ears and mind open. But most people have never analyzed just what it is they expect and need from the rituals they attend, so it's up to you as the liturgist to do some preliminary guesswork and use it to draw the members of your group into useful conversation. You'll need to be alert for hints of covert agendas among the membership and be ready, if necessary, to drag them (the agendas and ideas, not the members) out into the light. This is yet another reason for every liturgist to study the general subject of small-group dynamics.

Here are some suggestions to help you with your needs and expectations analysis:

Children

Kids generally find all religious ceremonies boring unless they are allowed some form of meaningful, *active* participation such as singing in a choir, being altar boys or girls, acting in ritual dramas, dancing, clapping their hands, or playing musical instruments, etc. Passive kinds of participation, such as picking flowers for the altar, drawing pictures to be used in the ritual, or making pottery tools to be used, are better than no participation at all, but not as exciting as the active kinds. Kids like ceremonies with lots of sound and color and action. They hate sermons (so do most adults) but love storytelling. Since effective religious and magical rituals always require the cooperation of everyone's inner child, some of these attitudes hold for older people as well.

This is why insisting on incorporating older children, say from seven to twelve years of age, in your liturgies, rather than banishing them to child care or Sunday school, will benefit the older members of your group—it will force you to develop liturgies that are exciting and interesting!

Teenagers

Teens can stand still longer than younger children and many are genuinely interested in magic and mysticism. Nonetheless, adolescent boys and girls "just wanna have fun"! Most teenagers go to religious ceremonies (when they go willingly) for social reasons: to meet other teenagers, to bond with their own gender, to engage in quaint mating customs, etc. Although they enjoy being able to actively participate, some will want to be parts of a group (such as a choir or a bunch of dancers), while others will prefer to perform solo. Most teenagers will insist that their participation be meaningful rather than obvious busywork, and will enjoy being given moderately challenging responsibilities in the ceremony. Of course, the more intelligent ones will expect you to explain why you do your ceremonies the way that you do, instead of the way that they would like to see them done.

One error that parents in many religions make is assuming that their teenaged kids will be happy about having a public coming-of-age ceremony. Puberty is generally an awkward and confusing experience and many adolescents would prefer to do such rites in private (if at all), or just with family members around. Yet I've seen Neopagan parents push their daughters into first-blood (menstruation) celebrations at public festivals, surrounding the teenagers with dozens of well-meaning strangers saying all sorts of embarrassing things to them. These women's mysteries rituals can be wonderful experiences, but not if the girls haven't been consulted first. Similar embarrassment can happen with boys going through a coming of age ceremony, either as part of a men's mysteries group or as an open ritual. When planning to include a teenager as an active participant, let alone as the star, of a ritual, always ask them first! Of course, if you've been preparing them for it from early childhood, they'll be less likely to object and more likely to be enthusiastic and proud.

Adults

Grownups have many of the same ceremonial concerns as kids and teenagers, but generally are also interested (some quite deeply) in the polytheological, theurgical, and thaumaturgical aspects of liturgy (as are some teens). Adults go to worship ceremonies hoping to receive such spiritual benefits as: direct communication with the divine, creative inspiration, psychological healing of themselves and others, strength to carry on with heavy burdens, courage in the face of adversity, new ideas and insights about the meaning of their lives, and greater understanding of the universe. They are also interested in such practical magical benefits as: physical healings, prosperity, fertility, attracting romance, improving their luck, saving the Earth, making governments more just, and helping the poor.

Adults like to participate in rituals, but most are not dedicated enough to want to take responsible roles during the ceremonies themselves, preferring to let others run the show while they concentrate on enjoying the experience. However, many such passive consumers of religion are happy to help in off-stage supporting roles, and will get a great deal of satisfaction out of seeing their flower arrangements on the altar, their embroidery in the vestments, their carpentry in the temple, their choreography being danced, their homemade incense being burned, etc. Such contributions to the overall liturgical experience are their way of offering sacrifices and should be encouraged and appreciated.

Seniors

Older folks have all the interests and concerns of adults, along with (usually) a deeper interest in matters relating to health and mortality. A person can enter this phase of life at any age from forty to eighty, depending upon when gray hair, fading sight, brittle bones, and other signs of bodily decay begin to manifest. Seniors develop an increasing philosophical and polytheological interest in the topic of mortality, which is why people suffering from other terminal diseases—extreme old age is one, after all—can also feel and function like seniors. But don't be too quick to label members of your congregation as belonging to this class—there are a sizable number of physically active sixty- and seventy-year-olds who think of themselves as middle-aged, and modern medicine may continue to increase their numbers and extend their longevity.

Seniors appreciate it when their life experience is valued, and often have a great deal of practical wisdom to share (along with some stubborn conservatism). They are often willing to take more responsibility in a group, and some retired folks are happy to find ways to fill the time once filled by their earlier occupations. When their health is frail, or various handicaps begin to appear, active physical participation in rituals may become more difficult and special arrangements may need to be made (see next chapter).

Since seniors expect liturgy to give them everything that it gave them earlier as adults, but also to communicate a strong sense of immortality, tradition, and continuity, liturgies that stress survival after death and spiritual immortality, and that show respect for the ancestors (whom they expect to eventually join), are going to be popular with elderly members of your congregation. When facing their own mortality, links to the past can imply a link to the future as well, which is why the historical precedent and affirmation of continuity parts of the liturgy are so important.§§ This attitude of "the faith will carry on even after I'm gone" appeals to many, giving them another type of immortality.

The Deities and Other Spirits

Thousands of years of religious documentation, as well as personal experience in those faiths where deities and other spirits show up regularly to converse with their worshippers, all suggest to us that they have their own expectations for your liturgies. They expect you to prepare a physical and psychic atmosphere that will be comfortable for them to visit, to invite them (through invocation or evocation) *properly,* according to custom and tradition, and to feed them appropriate amounts of mana in their preferred flavors. They also expect you to be properly prepared to receive their blessings, to have a clear idea of just what you want from them, and to thank them respectfully when they leave.

Specific deities, ancestors, nature spirits, and other entities may also have personal expectations: special food and drink to offer, special songs to sing or rhythms to drum, special actions to include or avoid, etc. Finding out about these individual preferences is an important part of your preparatory research and should never be neglected.

Books on mythology, comparative religions, history, archeology, and folklore are good sources for information on the preferences of divinities and other spirits (expect to have to screen out creedist and other cultural biases). Family diaries and reminiscences are good for finding out about ancestors, while biographies and autobiographies are handy when you plan to invite famous dead people to attend your rites.

Dead or alive, mortal or immortal, everyone (and every One) who participates in your liturgies is going to have her or his own needs and desires. With luck, imaginative questions, and a little research, you can figure most of these out. It's then up to you to incorporate ceremonial elements to accommodate them.

---

§§ See Chapter 3, Phase One and Phase Five.

5

PEOPLE WITH
SPECIAL NEEDS

Varieties of Participatory Handicaps

Not everyone who attends your rituals is going to be a perfect speci-
men of physical, emotional, and mental health, in the prime of their
life, and fully capable of participating in whatever activity your liturgical design has planned. Unless you plan to screen all your participants to exclude the "differently-abled" (the politically correct term
as of 2008 C.E.), and to banish others when they start to get old,
you will need to pay attention to the special needs that any expected
participants may have, and be prepared to make sudden changes if a
differently-abled person shows up at the last minute.

Where does the responsibility reside for identifying and articu-
lating a differing ability, need, or preference? Is it the responsibility
of the individual with special needs to express their concerns to the
group or its leader? Or should the group or leader take responsibility
for ascertaining such needs and always conduct ritual in such a way
that it is accessible to everyone as a matter of course? Yes.

As you will see in this chapter, the responsibilities are mutual.
Granted, one hopes that spiritually oriented groups and their leaders
are somewhat psychic, yet no one ever bats a thousand, and it is unfair
to expect them to guess unexpressed special needs that individuals

may have. Instead, groups and their leaders should make it clear to all participants that they are open to requests for changes based on special needs.

Here's a list of some of the major sorts of challenges that the participants in your liturgy may face:

Physical challenges

- Mobility impairment
- Allergies and asthma
- Chemical intolerance
- Height and weight differences
- Pregnancy
- Contagious diseases

Sensory challenges

- Vision problems
- Hearing problems

Mental challenges

- Dyslexia
- Right/left perception
- Counting impairment
- Understanding instructions
- Understanding intellectual content

Emotional challenges

- Physical contact intolerance
- Disfigurement
- Severe psychological disturbance

You are not likely to be able to come up with liturgical designs and performance customs that will handle every conceivable handicap that a participant may have. All these challenges have different effects on the ability to participate in ritual, so one set of alternatives isn't going to work for everyone. The more alternatives you have available for accomplishing each ritual activity, however, the more likely it is that a given need can be met.

The best that any ritual organizer or facilitator can do is to investigate the needs of your regular attendees, make provisions for the commonest sorts of challenges, and inquire at every pre-ritual briefing as to whether someone is there who has special needs.

Now let's look at these categories one by one.

Physical Challenges

Mobility impairment is by far the commonest physical challenge, and I'm not just talking about people in wheelchairs. Lots of people have difficulty walking long distances to a ritual site, standing for long (or even short) periods of time, participating in dances, and/or dodging other people who are moving rapidly. Transportation to the ritual site should be as easy as possible, and comfortable chairs (with arms, to facilitate sitting and rising) should be available in the ritual area (sitting on logs or stumps may be more painful than standing).

In some cases, these chairs can be placed in the center of the ritual area, perhaps with (or as) your musicians and/or with the small children during dances. Be aware, though, that the noise may be painful close-up and that kids rampaging around a small area can knock chair sitters over! You could also place chairs in an arc facing the main activity area (such as the altar and central fire), and consider such "elder's thrones" as a place of honor—but then you have to dance *very* carefully around them, if at all. Another option, depending upon the number of folks who need to sit and their ritual skills, is to make the chairs into special props, such as thrones at the four directions or behind the altar(s), and to give these chair sitters special duties in the liturgy.

If you were planning a procession to the ritual site, it's a good idea to have the mobility-impaired participants (along with musicians who have non-portable instruments, the fire watchers, etc.) stay at the ritual site. They can perform necessary preliminary steps such as lighting the fire(s), consecrating the altar and tools, leading a guided meditation for the other folks waiting, etc., until the procession appears. People could be stationed just outside of the ritual site to bless the processors as they arrive. All of this low-stress activity not only empowers the mobility impaired, it gets necessary pre-ritual tasks accomplished, and prevents the mana in the ritual site from being fragmented and chaotic during the wait for the procession. Above all, mobility impaired individuals should not be made to feel in the way and dumped someplace while everyone else does the "important stuff."

Incense, perfumes, scented oils, flowers, and wood smoke all have important aesthetic roles in many liturgies. But any and all of these can trigger allergies or asthmatic reactions, which can have subtle or devastating effects on the individual and on the ceremony. If you know that you have someone with allergic or asthmatic problems attending, you may be able to solve the problem by placing them upwind of the fire (or giving them encouragement to move their position as necessary), not censing/saging them or the people on either side, not anointing them with oil, etc. If their problems are severe, they may have to be resigned to watching the liturgy from a safe distance and/or forming their own group to do rituals without triggering ingredients.

If you are going to be using alcohol, tobacco, caffeine, sugar, or other mind-altering substances in your liturgy, you need to have alternate arrangements available for those participants who cannot tolerate them or who choose not to use them for spiritual reasons. Recovering alcoholics, ex-smokers, seniors with prostate problems, diabetics, people with eating disorders, etc., will all have good and sufficient reason to not consume one or more of these substances. It is now common for most Neopagan rituals to include two liquids to be blessed by the deity(ies), one alcoholic and the other non-alcoholic. Sugar-free food can be used for ceremonial meals, sage can be burned instead of tobacco (though some people are allergic to sage), etc. These situations require you to research who's likely to be showing up for your ritual, with what limitations, and then be imaginative in altering your liturgical design.

Height and weight differences can cause trivial but annoying problems for some. A person who is exceptionally tall or short will find it uncomfortable to hold hands or to have her/his arms around the persons on either side for long. People who are exceptionally overweight (or "differently horizontal," as Deborah Lipp puts it) may find it difficult to move gracefully in small areas and/or to dance vigorously. These people should be encouraged to modify their physical movements to meet their comfort needs.

Expectant mothers have very special needs. Most of what's been discussed above is relevant here: chairs should be present, incense should not be blown in their faces, nonalcoholic beverages should be available, etc. Use your common sense and be sure to ask every pregnant woman present if she wants or needs special attention (many don't).

One last physical challenge is having a contagious disease. If someone has an illness that is easily spread by sneezing or touch, they should stay home, of course (though you may still have a religious obligation to visit them). A disease that requires intimate contact to transmit, or the exchange of bodily fluids, on the other hand, is not necessarily cause to exclude anyone. Such folks should be advised that it's okay for them not to exchange kisses during a dance, that they don't have to touch other participants, and that they should bring their own cup or that one can be provided. In the latter situation, you merely pour consecrated fluids from a main cup into the individual's cup, thus preventing bacteria or viruses from being passed mouth-to-mouth. Some groups, especially during flu season, may prefer to have everyone bring their own cup and to consecrate and pass pitchers of wine, water, or whatever.

One common theme you may have noticed throughout this discussion of physical challenges is that vigorous dances, especially spiral dances or others that wind about the entire ritual area, are often a bad idea when physically- or sensory-challenged people are present.

Not only can small children and people in chairs get knocked over (along with altars and other props), but asthmatics and the obese will run out of breath, children and other short people can get their arms severely yanked, folks with foot or leg problems can trip and fall, etc. Dancing should either be left to the young and healthy and/or should be slow and stately, with plenty of care taken for those who need it.

SENSORY CHALLENGES

Sensory challenges each present their own needs. When considering visual problems it's important to remember that there is a wide variety of them that people can have. Some folks are near-sighted, far-sighted, have tunnel vision, lack depth perception, are color blind, etc., and some can see little or nothing at all.* Similarly, there are many sorts of hearing impairment. Some folks can hear only loud noises, others only those above or below a certain pitch, still others only out of one ear, etc.

To make your liturgy effective for these people you need to focus on two areas: personal safety and multisensory stimulation.

It's probably safest for most people with visual challenges (and some with hearing problems) to remain stationary throughout the ceremony, so the comments made above about the mobility impaired would apply here as well. Someone with normal vision should remain near the visually impaired to interpret as needed and to prevent others from colliding with them. A sign-language translator can be useful for the deaf and/or signing can be combined with ritual gestures to great artistic effect. A written outline of the rite, designed to be legible in the expected lighting conditions, can be very useful for hearing-impaired participants.

Multisensory stimulation means that all cues and ritual actions should be both visual and auditory, as well as kinesthetic (when possible).

---

* Although folks with the psychological equivalents of these problems can present even greater challenges to a ritual group.

You need that sort of approach to make a ritual as powerful as possible anyway, so the presence of vision- or hearing-impaired individuals should merely be an added inducement to make sure that every element of your liturgy reinforces every other one.

Mental Challenges

It's important not to assume that everyone attending your ritual can read a script, count to ten, tell left from right or clockwise from counterclockwise, or understand or remember instructions given several minutes before. I'm not talking here about people with low intelligence, but rather about a range of subtle mental impairments that can temporarily or permanently affect otherwise normal people. Your group may not be prepared to host people with severe mental handicaps (few congregations in any religion are, unfortunately), but you can and should be able to handle those with minor ones.

Dyslexia, left/right confusion, poor memory, etc. can be approached as challenges to you, the liturgist, to see to it that your prayer books (scripts) are typeset with large serif type and include graphics with arrows to show movement cues, that your liturgical structure flows smoothly and inevitably from one step to the next, that obvious cues and instructions to the participants are incorporated into the ritual design, and so forth.

People who can't understand the intellectual content of your ceremonies, whether because of age, mental impairment, lack of education, or language difficulties, must be reached through nonintellectual means such as music, song, storytelling, dance, drama, and the other arts. These can very frequently succeed in communicating ideas and experiences that straightforward speech and writing can't. Effective use of the arts will make your liturgies better experiences for everyone, as well as making them as inclusive as possible.

Emotional Challenges

Neopagans, even more than members of other liberal religions, tend to be a huggy-kissy crowd. Most of us love handholding, hugs, kisses, chain dances, and other sorts of physical contact, and we generally manage to work a lot of these into our ritual designs. Unfortunately, there are a sizable number of folks for whom even handholding is an ordeal. I'm not talking about people who are cold and distant sorts, but rather about those who are survivors of rape, incest, and various sorts of physical, emotional, and sexual abuse (although I suspect that some of the cold and distant are exactly such people). We now know that a high percentage of women and men have been victimized over the years and that all of our communities, Neopagan and mainstream, have many such people as members.

Meeting the needs of people who find physical contact unpleasant, without making them feel bad or spoiling the warm intimacy for the other participants, is not easy. If you know that people like this are present, you can suggest that they wear some special sign (such as a ribbon of a particular color, or a picture of a hand with a "No" circle and slash mark across it) during the ritual, and have plenty of the signs available. Such signs should be easily visible under your expected lighting conditions. Or you can suggest that they stand or sit in a special safe space during the liturgy, where everyone will know not to hug or kiss them.

Related to this issue is the problem that some people have with kissing and/or hugging members of their own or the opposite sex. Whether this constitutes a handicap or not I will leave up to the reader, but it's a good idea to develop customs in your group to deal with the issue. Heterosexual men in kissing dances, for example, will often just touch cheeks with (or nod pleasantly to) the other men, and women who do not want to be hugged by a particular person (or at all by a particular class of people) will often just squeeze the other person's arms below the shoulders and move quickly on. These issues of group and personal intimacy are important ones that should be discussed during your liturgical planning sessions.

Another emotional challenge, one that hits both its victims and its observers, is that of ugliness and physical disfigurement. Not everyone is pretty and the term "looksism" has been coined (I believe originally by the women's community) to refer to discrimination based on physical appearance. Whether we're talking about those who are differently horizontal, or who have had limbs amputated, bald men or bearded women, or those who have been scarred by fire or accident, the way that we or someone else looks can have psychological effects ranging from the trivial to the devastating.

It's vital that every individual be treated with the dignity that they deserve as human beings, yet you also need to pay attention to the effects that someone's presence may have on your ritual. This is one of the trickiest areas of ritual casting and performance—in fact, it's a spiritual, political, and psychological minefield. Normally, someone who is elderly and "ugly" should not be asked to play the role of a beautiful young divinity in a ritual drama. Yet if everyone knows and loves them as a member of their community, they may be transformed during the ritual and their inner beauty may shine forth.

On the other hand, someone with a severe disfigurement may come to your liturgy and shock the other participants so much that no one can concentrate on the ritual. Granted this is a rare occurrence, since most such people isolate themselves out of a justified fear of exactly such reactions. Here is where a quick conference with the person before the ceremony is vital. Welcome them, and then find out if they have any particular talent, such as singing, poetry, leading guided meditations, etc., which they would be willing to use in the liturgy. If so, draft them immediately, *even if you have to bump someone else from that role.* If not, assure them that they can participate as fully as they wish. The key point is to integrate them into the group and the ritual as matter-of-factly as possible. You may also wish to subtly modify your guided meditations to focus on the ideas of inner beauty and the importance of the individual soul, without making obvious references to the disfigured person's presence.

Of course, all this will be difficult if you suffer from looksism yourself, and will still require the members of your group to deal with their own prejudices and fears—especially if the new person decides to become a regular. That is a spiritual exercise I will leave for the reader.

Dealing with Spiritual Emergencies

People with severe psychological disturbances can present yet another sort of challenge. Someone who is suffering from severe schizophrenia or multiple-personality syndrome may begin to behave bizarrely in the middle of your ceremony. A particularly insecure person may try to hog attention. An incest survivor may suddenly start to have memory flashbacks. A self-destructive individual may decide to try and commit suicide with your ritual sword. A widow or widower may break down into uncontrollable grief.

Fortunately these sorts of events aren't common, but they are normal. A properly executed liturgy will raise and channel large amounts of emotion, and therefore of mana. Anyone who is on the edge of a psychological transformation, positive or negative, can be tipped over that edge by a strong mana flow. You therefore need to know how to handle such situations.

First, be ready to accept that your liturgy may indeed get ruined. The immediate psychological and spiritual needs of the individual will in some situations be obviously more important than keeping the ceremony running smoothly. After all, you can always do the ritual over later, but you can't undo a suicide or a psychotic break. Still, if you can, you should try to help the disturbed person in such a way as to allow the liturgy to continue.

Second, whoever in your group has had formal training in psychological counseling and spiritual first aid should go to the person and apply their skills. Everyone needs to be aware that what may seem like a mental or emotional breakdown may in fact be a moment of spiritual transformation for the individual involved (or not).[49]

The helper(s) should ascertain as quickly as possible the nature of the problem and the appropriate response. Perhaps your group should concentrate their mana on doing a healing; perhaps the person needs to be removed from the ritual area and given a cup of hot tea; perhaps they need to address a public prayer to the deity(ies) being worshipped; perhaps they've been possessed and need to communicate a message to the other participants; perhaps they're merely an egomaniac who needs to be firmly shushed! Generally it's better (spiritually and liturgically) to go along with their genuine needs, rather than to fight them.

Which is, of course, true of all the other special needs we've been discussing in this section. It's often a good idea to have one or more people assigned to the task of greeting newcomers, assisting those who are challenged in some fashion, and making sure that everyone is empowered and enabled to participate fully in the liturgy. That's part of what makes a group of isolated individuals into a community.

Better yet, make sure that people with special needs are invited into the liturgical planning process from the beginning. At the least, you can consider the liturgical participation of such people as a creative exercise in your planning, and be prepared to welcome them if, as, and when they arrive.

I am especially indebted in this chapter to the following folks for their ideas: Beket Asar of *Ár nDraíocht Féin:* A Druid Fellowship, Jade and Lynnie of the Re-formed Congregation of the Goddess, and Magenta Griffiths of Prodea Temple.

6

What, Where, When

The Nature of the Occasion

No matter how unique a particular situation may seem, the practicing liturgist will soon discover that almost all the rituals she/he needs to design can be seen as special cases within certain common overlapping categories of liturgy: those for personal and group needs, personal and group rites of passage, and rites of intensification (cyclical celebrations).

Rituals done for *personal and group needs* can be for inducing or attracting fertility, prosperity, love, healing, peace, general blessings, etc. An individual or group with a particular focus of activity may do ceremonies to achieve certain spiritual, ecological, social, economic, or political goals.

Personal rites of passage may include ceremonies for dedicating and protecting children, celebrating a coming-of-age, handfastings and weddings, ordinations, death watches, funerals, etc.

Group rites of passage are more likely to be such things as the dedication of a new hospital, school, temple, or sacred grove, the installation of new officers for the group, a change in the group's name or status, etc.

Rites of intensification will mark various important events that occur on a regular schedule, such as solstices and equinoxes, the Quarter Days (ancient European seasonal festivals), the phases of the moon, the beginning or end of local hunting, fishing, or harvesting seasons, etc.

Deciding which category(-ies) your ritual fits into will let you shape your liturgical design with greater clarity. Once you research how others have done similar rituals, you'll have new concepts and material to be absorbed and transmuted in your own design work. This is in the best tradition of creative eclecticism: steal any good ideas that don't run fast enough to get away!

Location, Location, Location

What sort of site will be used for your ceremony? Your choice will affect the physical, social, psychological, and magical aspects of your liturgy. It's better to choose a site to match the liturgical design, rather than vice versa, but often you must simply work with what's available.

If you're going to be working outdoors, private land is generally better than public, since you're less likely to be disturbed by tourists, hunters, or park rangers. However, if your group is seeking new members, doing a few ceremonies in city parks, especially near universities, can attract folks who might otherwise never hear of you. It can also attract trouble, so make sure that security precautions are taken to prevent disruption. It's also essential to find out from the people who control the land (whether members of your religious community or the city parks department) just what their rules are concerning hours, fires, alcoholic beverages, numbers of people, etc. If your congregation won't agree to those rules, you'll need to choose a different site. If insurance will be needed, you'd better find out early, as getting it can take several days or weeks and may require you to ask for donations before the event.

Pay attention to noise levels and acoustics, whether indoors or out. If there are railroad tracks, a fire station, a hospital, or an airport nearby, you can expect loud noises to occur at random intervals. These can drown out invocations and music, destroying both the concentration of the participants and whatever patterns of mana have been created. Cute comments or jokes about "Let's just pretend it's a dragon" or "As we were saying..." won't repair the damage. If you're working indoors in such a location, you should make every effort to physically soundproof the room. Of course, a half hour spent investigating the neighborhood could prevent most such problems.

If you are stuck with a potentially noisy location, one technique that *has* worked well in large rituals is to tell the participants beforehand that noisy interruptions may occur and that everyone should relax, not fight it, and softly chant "Aum" (or some other one-word mantra) over and over again when this happens, until the outside noise dies away and the people leading the ritual continue.

As for acoustics, it's a good idea when inspecting a proposed site to do some shouting, singing, whispering, drumming, harp playing, or other noise-making equivalent to what your ceremony will require. See how far the sounds carry, what the echoes are like, if details are lost at a distance, etc. Then you can decide if you want to use the location at all and if so, whether you'll need sound amplification equipment, louder acoustic instruments, etc. The number of people to be present will affect the acoustics as well, dampening much sound with the white noise of normal breathing, coughing, shuffling, etc., and blocking some of the sound with their bodies.

If the weather is likely to be foul, or there are members of your group who can't handle being outdoors long during the winter, and you don't own your own temple building, you should try to find, borrow, or rent some sort of appropriate space. I know this isn't always easy, but trying to fit thirty people into a small living room can be just as difficult, and far less aesthetically pleasing. If you are planning an outdoor ceremony, but you don't trust the weather forecast for your scheduled date, you should have an alternate indoor location readily available (and vice versa) and your liturgical design should be adaptable to the change. Make sure that your announcements mention both locations and set an alternate time sufficiently after the originally planned time to allow people to get from one site to the other. If the alternate site gets used, try to post a notice to this effect at the original location.

How do you get an indoor location? If you own some land, you may be able to find a large cave, or build a cabin, yurt, or longhouse. A half-dozen determined people can create one of these in a month, just working on weekends (see your local public library for instruction books). In six months you could build a rough duplicate of the Scandinavian stave churches, which are believed by some scholars to have originally been the same design that was used for Paleopagan Norse temples.

Many public parks, even in large cities, have rustic-looking lodges, often with fireplaces, that your group can rent. These are usually surrounded by trees, and can be ideal for medium to large groups. Masonic and other fraternal organizations, as well as liberal churches such as the Unitarian Universalists, are often willing to rent out local meeting space to members of minority belief systems.

Whether you're working in one of these lodges, your own temple, a living room, or someone's garage, set up the site to look as dramatic and non-mundane as possible. Theatrical set design will give you useful ideas for incorporating drapery, dramatic lighting techniques, etc.

Whether indoors or out, don't assume that your site needs to be circular. Paleopagans around the world had temples in the shapes of circles, rectangles, ovals, doubled squares, and odd polygons. As for groves of trees, where many of the Indo-European Paleopagan ceremonies took place, the average one is not a precise circle. Although it's aesthetically and democratically pleasing to have the congregation stand around in a circle, and this is the pattern with which most Neopagans are familiar (thanks to Gerald Gardner*), you can do effective group worship and/or magic using other geometrical shapes. You could try having your ceremonies with the people in a triangle, or in a square, or in lines facing a particular direction.

If you insist for religious reasons on working in a circle, try to make it as small as possible so you don't lose the benefit of everyone being able to make eye contact with one another. Concentric rings of people can work well, but only if the short people are in front, or the surface they are standing on is tiered.†

---

* See BEGWW.

† I find myself wondering if this is why so many Neolithic monuments had rings of raised earthworks around them.

Consider the theatrical difficulties as well as the mana patterns likely to be generated by your shape choices. For example, those of you with theater experience will agree that working "in the round" can be far more difficult than working in front of the observers. Unfortunately, with the latter setup, you may have problems with people who are unhappily reminded of childhood experiences in mainstream religions, and who may be unable to overcome their biases. It also tends to promote a performers vs. audience perception among the participants, instead of unity.

Up to a point, the larger the site you have, the better. You want enough room for the members of the congregation to stand, sit, or lie in whatever geometrical pattern you have chosen, while still leaving some empty space outside of them. However, if you're working indoors, you don't want a small group working in the middle of a gigantic room, since this tends to breed a sense of isolation and weakness. The acoustics of a very large room will also tend to dilute people's voices and other sounds, thus draining a lot of dramatic power. However, if you don't know for sure how many people to expect, err on the side of larger space.

Outdoors, shade can be an important factor, especially during the hotter months. Since a worship rite can last an hour or more, you need to make arrangements not only for shade, but for the health of the members of your congregation as well (providing water, hand fans, hats, seats, etc.). Humidity and wind will affect fires, papers, costumes, and altar tools (see the next few sections).

As we discussed in the last chapter, outdoor rituals can be very difficult for folks to attend if they are blind or mobility impaired, unless you have volunteers ready to assist them. If you're expecting people to show up in wheelchairs, make sure your site is accessible.

Even people who are not physically handicapped may have difficulty arriving at your site if it's not near public transportation, or doesn't have sufficient parking space or bicycle racks nearby. Some people will refuse to go to a ceremony that requires driving a private car, simply on ecological principles. Others won't go anywhere that doesn't have a parking lot. These are yet more reasons why you should know your group well.

Finally, if you're going to go to a rural area, park your cars or bicycles, and then hike a mile to the actual ritual site, you'll probably need a liturgical design that's easy on props (especially heavy ones).

Finding the perfect spot to do your rituals can be a long, frustrating job, but it's worth it. Eventually you'll discover what every other religion in modern history has found out: having your own land, with buildings, trails, and other facilities to fulfill the needs of your congregation, is the best long-term solution.

Costumes and Props

Yes, we need to use those terms. You don't think all the funny clothes that a priest, rabbi, minister, choir director, or imam wears aren't ceremonial costumes? Just so, the cups, scrolls, staves, and other ritual tools that will see service in a liturgy are, on their most basic level, theatrical props designed to make it easier to direct the flow of emotional and spiritual energies. While specific historical, traditional, and (poly)theological concerns may be involved in the design and manufacture of these religious costumes and props, you can be sure that the designers and craftspeople are also paying attention, however covertly, to the theatrical impact of their resulting products. Just look at a few catalogs in your local religious supply shops!

Many decisions involving costumes and props will be based on those made about aesthetics and cultural focus (see next chapter), since you'll want people to use ceremonial tools and to wear clothing in the colors, fabrics, and styles that fit with the aesthetics and cultures you have selected. But here too, you may be forced to work within already established constraints. If the group of people for whom you are creating the ritual all have robes that touch the ground, and you had planned on having a procession over rough or muddy ground, the costumes or the choreography will have to be changed. If their sleeves are long and flowing, don't create parts of the ritual that involve reaching across a fire or an altar with easily knocked-over items (for example, anything taller than it is wide). If none of the members have staves, and there's no time to make some (let alone train anyone in their use), then don't plan a ritual combat using staves.

Bright colors, or at least ones that stand out from the other colors present, are a big help in making costumes visible. Decorations on the clothing can help to distinguish roles as well. Someone with a big harp embroidered, painted, or appliquéd on her/his robe is likely to be seen as a bard (or at least as a musical person). Someone with antlers on his hat or a bright gold sun on her cape will be assumed to be clergy and/or to be playing a role in a ritual drama—especially if most of the others present are not so decorated. If all your cupbearers are wearing similar clothes and wreaths of appropriate foliage in their hair, their coordinated movements will be much more dramatic.

Consider the use of tabards as a regular solution to costuming needs. These are rectangles of cloth sewn together at two corners (on the narrow sides) and worn over the shoulders. Two or three sizes will fit almost anyone and they can be decorated in a variety of ways for particular roles or occasions, then thrown over other clothing—even mundane secular clothing—to provide an instant ceremonial effect. Some congregations choose to make multiple tabards available for guests, so that everyone can be dressed in a way conducive to group identity.

The use of bright colors, as well as size factors, applies to props as well. If everyone will be two or three yards away from the main action, then small earthy-colored props may work just fine. But if some of the congregation are going to be twenty or thirty yards away, a brightly colored staff should be used instead of a plain wand, for example, and a one-quart, polished metal cup instead of a half-pint, unpainted pottery one.

The necessity for distinctive costumes and props to be maximally visible is one of the many reasons why precious metals (both real and fake) are so often used in their construction. Shiny stuff simply shows up better!

There are other aspects to props that should be considered, however. Many Neopagan liturgists create rituals that require standard

Wiccan ritual tools—pentacles, chalices, wands, and knives—without having any real reason for those tools to be there, and without any clear idea of how these tools can or should be used for dramatic or magical effect. When in doubt about whether or not a given prop is really needed, *skip it.* Unused or misused ceremonial tools merely clutter up the scene, and either add nothing to, or sometimes actively detract from, the quality of your liturgy.

Written materials are another problematic factor in liturgy. If something simply *has* to be read in a ritual, transfer the text to an attractive manuscript book or a scroll, calligraphed or else printed neatly according to the expected lighting conditions and the eyesight of those who will be reading it. This usually means that the object should be medium-sized to large, not small, and the reading of it should be handled as a dramatic element, not an offhand convenience for someone who can't remember lines.

Of course, some of us *do* have poor memories, so an outline of the liturgy can be handy to have available during the ceremony. Putting the words in runes, ogham letters, or another non-vernacular alphabet on banners or wall decorations can be very helpful without being *too* obvious. Cue cards, however, are simply tacky and should be avoided whenever possible. If they are unavoidable, disguise them.

One of the duties of a liturgist is to make up a complete props and supplies list for the organizers of the event to use early in their planning. The people purchasing and/or constructing these items should also keep track of the money and time required, as an aid to planning future ceremonies.

Altars

A major prop, yet one that most folks don't consider much, is the altar. What sort, if any, will your design require?

For European-oriented Neopagans, the whole question of altars is on weak historical ground. Some of the Western Indo-Europeans seem to have used stone altars inside or in front of their temple buildings, but we don't know for sure if altars were used in the sacred groves.

Among the ancient Hindus, however, who may well retain the old-est Indo-European customs, altars were vitally important, not just as ritual props but as religious symbols of territorial rule. Fire altars for Agni (the God of Fire and of Priesthood) were built with 360 stones and 360 bricks, representing the days of the year. The construction of each altar was considered (as were the subsequent sacrifices upon it) to restore or "reassemble" Prajapati, the primordial being who cre-ated the universe, and who had been exhausted over the course of the preceding year[50]. Without a properly constructed and consecrated al-tar, these public sacrifices simply could not be performed.

Such metaphysical considerations may not be important in your group's polytheology. Nonetheless, altars are useful for storing the ceremonial tools and supplies, as well as keeping them within easy reach during the rite, and make a good focus of dramatic attention when needed. I recommend them highly.

If you own your own land, your group might choose to build a permanent stone altar, designing it so a fire can be built upon or inside it. If you use public land, you can either plan on bringing your own altar, or on putting one together on-site from available rocks, stumps, etc. The challenge in the first case is to make your portable altar both sturdy and lightweight, in the second to wind up with something rea-sonably level at a convenient height (wedges can solve this problem).

How many altars should you have, and where should they be?

One near the center will do for most situations, and will tie in with archetypal images of the ritual center. Some denominations of Neopaganism prefer the single altar near the southern or western inside rim of a ritual circle (with the clergy thus facing north or east over the altar). When working in a rectangular sacred space, with the clergy facing the congregation, you'll probably want an altar to be front and center. The Western tradition seems to be to have it in the eastern part of the space.

However, you might consider having more than one altar. Neopa-gan Druids, for example, could create three small altars (for the three worlds of Land, Sea, and Sky, or for the nature spirits, the ancestors, and the deities), set in a wide triangle around a central one. *If* you decide that the four directions are important, you might choose to have small altars, shrines, or cairns (ceremonial rock piles) marking each compass point around the edges of the site.

The size of your altar(s) should fit with the overall size of your ritual space and the number of people who will be involved as clergy and congregation. The larger your ritual space, the larger your altar can be without people tripping over it, and the larger an altar you are likely to need—to hold all the tools necessary for serving a large congregation as well as to serve as a dramatic focus of attention. In a nine-foot diameter circle, the altar should be no larger than two feet across, and the clergy may well be part of the ring of people. An eighteen-foot diameter circle, however, could have a three-foot diameter altar with clergy around it, and a ring of people surrounding them.

By the way, if you live in an area with many fundamentalists, it may be a good idea to disguise any permanent altars as something else, since conservative monotheists have a bad habit of desecrating the sacred objects of competing faiths. If you want to have an outdoor sanctuary in fundamentalist territory, be sure that its function is not obvious to people who think that freedom of religion is a subversive, demonic plot.

FIRE

Fire is such an important element of ritual that many people don't feel that they have actually done a ceremony if no fires were present. It's no accident that the one bit of ritual that almost all Unitarian Universalist congregations perform willingly, despite the strong anti-liturgical bias many of their members may hold, is the "Lighting of the Chalice."[51] From the smallest candle to the largest bonfire, open flames are an almost universally recognized symbol of the divine. Using fire in your rites can add drama and wonder, but must be done very carefully to achieve the best (and safest!) results.

Indoors, you can usually use candles, placing them in sturdy, stable, fireproof candleholders on insulated surfaces. If you put candles at the four directions, make sure that they are not likely to be kicked over or blown out by people moving rapidly nearby, nor capable of setting people's robes on fire. Try putting them in large glass holders (such as the "hurricane" sort), or on tall candle-stands outside the ritual area, or hanging by chains from the ceiling, or in wall sconces.

Outdoors, candles don't usually work very well unless they are in enclosed glass or metal lamps or similar protective devices, since even the slightest breeze can blow out a small flame. Outdoors, candles should be pre-lit for two-three minutes before the rite to ensure proper burning. For processions or for marking the outer edges of sacred spaces, oil lamps or garden ("tiki") torches work best.

Indoors or out, inside your sacred space (unless it's very large), you're better off having a single place of fire, usually near the center, to serve as a focus of attention. This can be a large bonfire, small campfire, a cauldron filled with flammable materials, a candelabra, etc., depending on the size of your ritual area. Indoors, the fire will usually be on top of the altar itself, so pay attention to the flammability of the items (including any altar cloths) close to it. Outdoors, don't have your altar too close to a large fire.

Matches or already burning candles are much more dramatic as a flame source if you need to light something during your ceremony, but a working butane lighter should always be available near the altar or in someone's pocket. The long campfire sort are best, if practiced with beforehand. Have tongs, a trivet, and perhaps a hot pad nearby.

All fires produce light, heat, and smoke. The light of the flames will not be as dramatic in the daytime, so if you are working under bright lighting conditions, make your fire as large as is safely possible, to the point where you get the effect you wanted. The flammability factor already mentioned will be changed by the heat of the fire, which in turn depends in large part upon the nature of the fuel—one reason why rubbing alcohol is a favorite indoor ritual fire fuel: it burns at a low temperature and makes a lovely blue flame (which can be colored differently by adding various chemicals). Incense or paper thrown into a ritual fire can fill a room with smoke quickly (and won't work well with an alcohol fire). Experienced campers know that green wood produces far more smoke than dry wood, so don't use it indoors except in very small quantities.

Not only is too much smoke a health hazard for many people (asthmatics, for example), it is irritating, and thus distracting to everyone, especially if it causes the clergy, singers, or dancers to start coughing in the middle of an otherwise smoothly-flowing ceremony. Screaming smoke alarms and arriving fire engines can also mar the experience for many.

Fires are not only unpredictable in terms of burning too much; they are also prone to refuse to burn when you want them to. That's why you will usually want to make sure that your outdoor fires are started at least fifteen minutes before the ritual starts (unless lighting a bonfire is supposed to be a high point of the rite), and that any incense charcoals (church charcoal, not barbecue briquettes) are lit five or ten minutes beforehand.

Inspect and test your materials long before the ritual: How green or dry is the wood? How much alcohol should you put in the cup? Are the wicks trimmed on the tapers you are going to hand out? Is there oil in the lamps? Will the incense burn properly? Does your lighter have fuel? Are your matches really dry? Does your new design for a bonfire actually stay lit? Fruitlessly fighting with a fire that will not burn can wreck an otherwise excellent ritual. Pyrotechnicians and others who enjoy getting special effects with fires are usually as proud as any other artists, but serious ones will rehearse if asked.

Have at least one person in your group prepared with the correct training and tools to calmly handle any fires that threaten to get out of control. That person could be the same person who is responsible for lighting the fire. If she or he tells you that some of your fire plans are dangerous, *listen to them!*

Hotel owners or park rangers may have a temporary or permanent "Absolutely No Fires" policy at your site. You'll want to make sure that the policy really is official and is enforced with all religious groups, not just minority belief systems, but be prepared with alternate sources of illumination. Some very realistic battery-powered or electric artificial candles, from tea lights to pillars, are available. Combined with red and orange cloths, perhaps with small wind or fog machines, these candles can look like a small fire on an altar top. In no-fire zones, a warming plate might be used to gently melt perfumed wax. Though this won't produce dramatic smoke as burning incense would, it does produce the desired aromas, stimulating participants' sense of smell without open flames.

Timinɢ

Deciding the exact date and time of your ceremony will affect everything else in your liturgical design and execution. This requires you to balance both magical and mundane factors. The magical factors have to deal with the fact that different times of day, and different days of the year, have different energy patterns (physical, psychological, social, and thus magical) associated with them. So it may be easier or more difficult to accomplish a particular magical or religious goal at the specific time chosen.

Why should this be? Gribbin and Plagemann[52] demonstrated that the positions of the planets in the solar system cause significant, predictable changes in solar weather and sunspot patterns. These in turn affect earthly weather patterns, especially the ionization of the atmosphere, which the authors believe can trigger earthquakes. Certainly research has shown that the proportion of positive to negative ions in a given location can have profound effects on human and other animal mood swings. These patterns of ionization change from season to season, as do the proportions of light and darkness, which are also known to have strong psychological effects.

The daily solar cycle thus causes the mana available for use to be different at sunrise, noon, sunset, and midnight, and the halfway points between each. Similarly, because of the yearly solar cycle, the mana available at the solstices, equinoxes, and *their* halfway points are also unique. This is one of the reasons the Neopagan once-every-six-weeks holiday pattern is popular.

The phases of the moon can also have profound effects (ask any cop, ambulance driver, or psychiatric nurse about full moons!), especially when the moon is above the horizon. Readers who have a background in astrology will need no persuasion in this department, and will probably also consider the daily positions of the planets (and the transits they form to the natal charts of the leading participants) to be worth examining when selecting a date and time. The rest of you will have to experiment in order to verify my statements.

Pay attention to the biorhythms of the presiding clergy, to see if any of them will be having a critical day on the date selected (and then make plans to accommodate that fact).

In my experience, performing even a simple celebration of a Holy Day on the exact day of the year, and at the exact (or at least the symbolic) time of the day associated with the event being celebrated will dramatically multiply the ease and efficiency of your working.

Unfortunately, it's not easy to get people to show up for a ritual being held at an inconvenient time. Often the date you might believe to be the proper one for a Holy Day is in the middle of the civil week, and the time associated with the event may be very late at night, or in the middle of the working day.

However, you can give yourself some flexibility in the choice of a time of day, since you can choose to schedule your rite for either the astronomical or the symbolic instant of the event. For example, the spring equinox might occur on March 20th, at 10:15 pm in your local time zone. You could do your equinox ritual at 10:00 pm, or at the following sunrise (since sunrise is the time of day symbolically associated with the spring equinox). At the very least, you should schedule your ceremony sometime during the twenty-four hours surrounding the event.

This, however, often turns out to be a counsel of perfection. If you are planning a large public celebration, you'll have to schedule it according to the convenience of the majority of your group's members and guests. This usually means that you'll be stuck with the weekend before or after the event. Even so, try to do it at the appropriately symbolic time of day. For example, a Midsummer's Day celebration held at 9:00 PM is simply not as psychologically effective as one done at high noon. If you want to do a nocturnal ceremony, you can always make it the Eve of the Holy Day (at least if you're working with Indo-European holidays).

Don't forget such mundane matters as the work and child-care schedules of the members, local transportation patterns, meals, expected weather, fluctuating noise levels at the site, availability of facilities at different dates and times, etc. All of these have an impact on how many people show up, and on how well they enjoy themselves.

The trick is to balance genuine needs in the lives of your congregation against the laziness and inertia of those who simply haven't made attending your ritual a high priority. Remember that if you decide to do a fall equinox rite at sunset, you will probably not be able to get the sun to delay setting while latecomers straggle in.

7
How, Mundane

Formality vs. Informality

How formal or informal your liturgy should be may seem, at first, to be more of an aesthetic decision than anything else. After all, some folks like their rituals to be High Church Episcopagan[53] and others prefer to get down and get funky. Yet there are some technical considerations involved.

The word *formal* implies a concern with both structure and custom. Since all rituals have some sort of structure (whether competent or not), the question of formality within liturgy is one of (a) how conscious the structure is, (b) how tightly the structure is *maintained*, in both design and performance, and (c) how similar a given performance is to the traditionally ideal way(s) of doing it. Formality does not *necessarily* have anything to do with pomposity, verbosity, or a lack of humor.

In the Neopagan community, our custom has usually been to be *in*formal. Some of the reasons traditionally offered for this custom are more plausible than others. For example, many Neopagans tend to think of Native American, African, and other Paleopagan rituals as being informal, whereas the mainstream Jewish or Christian rituals are seen as having been formalized to the point of fossilization. Since it's the former kind of religion that inspires us, it makes sense that we would equate Paleopagan informality with authentic spiritual expression, and mainstream formality with everything else we happen to dislike about those religions. What many people don't realize is that Paleopagan ceremonies are usually *very* formal, both in terms of their structures and the customs associated with them. It's our Western upbringing that conditions us to equate physically active, rapidly paced ceremonies with informality.

But there are less honest reasons to reject formality in ritual. Most have to do with an unwillingness to admit just how difficult it can be to create and perform a formal ritual successfully. Ceremonies that require talent, training, discipline, and hard work from their participants are simply not going to be as popular among the lazy as those that can be done instantly by anyone, anywhere.

Let's explore some of the aspects that affect the formality factor. For example, what's the intelligence and vocabulary level of the clergy and congregation you are designing a ritual for? Formal ceremonies (if mostly spoken—see next section) usually have a higher verbal complexity than informal ones, and can be more difficult for unintelligent or uneducated people to perform or comprehend. As mentioned before, allowing for this factor can get you into *big political and social trouble*. Not doing so, however, can damage the precision of your mana flow, when parts of your group don't understand what you're saying and other parts are offended because you're "talking down" to them.

Formal ceremonies also require greater dramatic and musical skills from the clergy and bards, especially if the rite is going to be repeated on a frequent basis. The dangers of boredom should not be ignored. If your rituals bore the congregation—or even the clergy!—they're not going to raise a lot of mana. That means they're not going to enable the participants to do any significant thaumaturgical or theurgical work. On the other hand, the familiarity that bores some people gives a great deal of psychological comfort to others, and adds to the affirmation of continuity effect* while creating useful patterns of mana in the collective unconscious. Thus, the "custom" aspect of formality is a two-edged blade.

---

* See Chapter 3's discussion of Phases One and Five.

What happens if you need to create a liturgy on the spot, with no chance to do a detailed analysis of the situation? If you've developed your intuition along with your ritual skills, you'll be able to create what you need as you go. Ad hoc ceremonies are often *perceived* as informal, because the structure being invented during the ritual is an unconscious one. But if you string together bits and pieces of ritual with which your group is already familiar, and you invent a pattern that is appropriate to the occasion, you may wind up with a very formal, but nonetheless intuitive, rite.

In general, the larger your congregation, the more formality is needed to maintain the group mind's unity and focus in timing and imagery. It's important, however, to remember the difference between formality and pomposity. Here's one clue: are the clergy focusing more attention on the ceremony and the spirits invoked, or on themselves as being important people? This is where I reverse my favorite saying: *Competence is not a substitute for sincerity, either.*

Verbal Mode

Will your ceremony be mostly spoken, sung, or silent? Spoken ceremonies are certainly the easiest, and can give you precise fine-tuning of the mana flow, but they tend to get very long-winded (and thus boring) unless delivered with real dramatic skill. Having everything chanted and/or sung will boost a verbal ritual to the maximum, since the sounds of the chanting, singing, and incidental music will add their own subconscious power to that of the words. Having all the speeches in poetic forms that match the aesthetic and cultural themes of the ritual will add greatly to the power of your rite—*if* they are performed well.†

Poetry and songs also have the advantage of being easier to memorize than straight text. This means that a liturgy can be done without a script on the altar, and without the participants shuffling pieces of paper when they should be concentrating on generating and focusing mana.

---

† See Chapter 8.

If the clergy, bards, and congregation understand the liturgical design of the ceremony they are performing, they will be able to ad-lib any lines they might forget (though this is easier with prose than with poetry). The person who wrote the script might get his/her feelings hurt when some of their immortal words are skipped or changed, but the results of such ad-libs are sometimes better than the original wording.

The script for a greatly altered or brand-new liturgy can be placed discretely on the altar for the presiding clergy to glance at as needed. A poet or songwriter, who has just created a new work that she or he is going to perform as a part of the ceremony, can carry a cue card—or better yet, a scroll—in their pocket. A hearing-impaired participant may be given a copy of the script (or even just the outline) to help him/her follow the rite. But other than these exceptions, paper should be avoided during a worship ritual.

Yes, I know that some religions require a script on the altar, or in the hands of the clergy, at all times. But this custom exists precisely because they fear the change and evolution in their rituals that incomplete memorization and subsequent ad-libs might create. If a religion supposedly has the one true right and only way, then any deviation, growth, or evolution in their ceremonies will be viewed as spiritually dangerous to their members, and/or politically and economically to the religion's leaders. Fortunately, members of liberal religious traditions do not have this limit on their creativity.

Another verbal mode you might choose to use is that of *call and response,* where a clergyperson says something and the congregation responds in a quasi-conversational manner. Call and response can create a very powerful back-and-forth flow of energy between the clergy and the congregation, and will aid in unifying the group mind. Litanies as used in the Catholic churches, for example, are a tightly controlled form of energy flow, gaining their effectiveness more from their hypnotic repetition than from the amount of mana they raise. On the other hand, the classic African-American church style of call and response, is based on ancient and effective West-African Paleo-pagan methods, and can generate a lot of mana.

When writing call and response material, by the way, be careful not to ask questions that may elicit a disruptive response (no easy task).

You *can* do ceremonies partly or completely in silence, or with only nonverbal sounds. These require the same sorts of nonverbal dramatic skills that a mime uses, and will work best with a smaller group (at least for entire rituals). For ritual drama inserted into a large-scale ceremony, however, the art of mime can be very effective.[54]

Movement Mode

Kinesthetics also need to be considered. Will your rite be physically dynamic or static? If there is going to be a lot of moving back and forth across the ritual site, passing of objects around, dancing, etc., then you need a flat, clear, and level site, with room to move in, and you need to train your people in these movements. If either such a site or the necessary training is unlikely, you should change your design to one in which the participants can stand or sit most of the time, and/or change the movements to slow, simple ones. Watch out for the boredom problem again, and be aware that for some members of your congregation, staying in one position for long periods of time may be physically painful or even impossible.‡

Many Neopagan rites require dancing by the majority of the congregation, but very few modern Westerners actually know *how* to do group dancing. Holding hands and skipping (or more usually, stumbling) around in a circle is *not* dancing, especially when it's done without any true involvement in the movement. The spiral dances that have become a required activity at many Neopagan ceremonies are usually disorganized, chaotic, and frequently painful and dangerous to the very young and the mobility impaired. Ecstatic dancing, especially when done by adults wearing animal costumes, can create a situation where small or slow participants are stepped on or poked by sharp costume parts.

---

‡ See Chapter 5, "Physical Challenges."

Fortunately, there are ways to learn safe and effective ritual dance techniques. Local folk dance, square dance, and medievalist societies often have free or inexpensive classes available. These can teach the basic steps to some ritually useful dances in only a few sessions. Those who want to dress as spirit animals might consider joining a morris dance team. If the members of your group are unwilling to attend such classes, you should probably skip dancing as part of your design.

You can confine movement to slow walks; perhaps having a more complex dance performed by a talented few. Almost everyone can learn to walk rhythmically, clap their hands, raise and lower their arms, etc. Ecstatic dances can be limited to the healthy and spry. That way, neither children nor the elderly members of your congregation will be endangered.

Dramatic Tension, Humor, Play, and Pacing

Good drama always involves some uncertainty on the part of the audience: Will the Winter Solstice sun actually return? Will the May Queen wed the Green Man? Is the Corn King really dead? No matter how familiar the participants are with the story, they should experience at least a moment or two of uncertainty.[55]

As the liturgist, you have the task of inserting uncertainty into the ritual in such a fashion as to facilitate rather than disrupt the mana flow. For example, in the old Reformed Druids of North America rituals, after the sacrifice (leaves and twigs from a tree) was offered, the presiding clergy asked the four winds whether the sacrifice had been accepted or not. A stiff breeze, a sudden birdcall, or other omen was expected (and usually received). In the summer half of the year the clergy would declare that all was well, but in the winter half the sacrifice would be announced as unaccepted. This worked well as a way to introduce controlled dramatic tension, except for the tiny fact that sometimes the omens would not *behave* properly (showing up when they weren't supposed to, or not appearing when they should). This disturbed some folks.

In the early versions of the Druid liturgy I created for *Ár nDraíocht Féin:* A Druid Fellowship[56], this request for an omen of sacrificial acceptability was done to see if the *praise offerings* (music, poetry, songs, etc.) sacrificed were acceptable to the deity(ies) of the occasion. If the answer were negative, then we would do more praising. The plan was that if we got three refusals of the praise offerings, then we would skip to the last phase of the ritual. We never received three refusals, but, unfortunately, we discovered that some members of the grove were saving their best material for use on a second or third round, rather than giving their all each time! This somehow seemed rude to us.

Eventually we changed how the omen taking worked. We now assume that the deities are willing to accept the sacrifices we offer (since many of them haven't been getting much in the way of offerings for centuries). So we throw the ogham sticks or runes (or do some other form of culturally appropriate divination) to see what sort of responsive blessings the deity(ies) has/have in mind for us. Sometimes we use the received omens to tune, omit, or even completely replace our intended thaumaturgical or theurgical workings.

In this fashion drama, which came out of the temple, goes back to its religious origins. We can't, however, afford a contrived solution to every uncertainty in a worship ritual, though this is normal in mundane theatrical presentations. If we actually believe in the deities we worship, then we have to be willing to accept that sometimes their answers to us will be different from what we wanted or expected— and we have to be prepared to deal with such answers.

How does humor fit into all this? *Very carefully.* I have seen humor used in ceremonies with positive results on several occasions, both as theatrical inserts in large-scale liturgies, and as quiet quips to bring back a congregation's focus after a minor disruption of the mana flow. I've also seen it used, often deliberately, to drain the power from rituals that are getting too heavy for the jesters (sometimes the clergy themselves!) to handle. Humor is a two-edged blade that should be handled with the greatest of care, or left out entirely.

I *don't* recommend invoking Trickster deities, such as Loki or Coyote, let alone deities associated with chaos (such as Eris), into a modern ceremony, unless like Legba/Exu they are also gatekeepers. These entities have a habit of destroying any nontraditional rituals at which they actually show up. Most of them have a nasty streak to their characters—especially Eris, who has become a *fun* deity only in the last thirty years[57]. They need to be handled with the greatest of care and respect, using the techniques that have been developed over the centuries by the people who originally worshipped them. Unfortunately, the vast majority of people who invoke these deities, whether formally or informally, do so in order to provide a convenient excuse for poor liturgical design, preparation, and/or performance.

All this does not mean that you can't have a sense of play in your liturgies. Play is a very important human activity[58] and there are many occasions when playful elements are perfectly appropriate in a worship ceremony. If you are invoking deities who are associated with childhood or adolescence, for example, playfulness can fit well into the emotional patterns of your rite. Parental deities are often playful when interacting with their worshippers and an acknowledgment of this is often appropriate, especially if they are pulling gentle tricks on us. Bacchus, Dionysus, or other rowdy divinities often enjoy having their worshippers play games and get silly.

However it is usually *not* appropriate to insert playfulness into liturgies designed to worship deities associated with death, hunting, war, asceticism, etc. Healing deities, on the other paw, are sometimes serious, sometimes playful, and a small bit of humor and play is often helpful when doing a healing spell, especially if the sick person is present.

Pacing is something that anyone familiar with the theater will tell you is absolutely crucial to the success of a performance. A liturgy should be designed and performed with each segment flowing smoothly into the next. You don't want segments to either slow down to the point where everyone gets bored and their attention begins to wander, nor to speed up to the point where people lose track of what's happening. A five-minute, guided meditation may be too long for some groups, too short for others. Taking thirty seconds to bless each person in turn is fine if you have only a small group, but can be a disaster with a large one. A chant that naturally builds to a peak in three minutes should not be dragged out for ten. The only way to learn pacing is to experiment a lot with modular ritual design§ and to rehearse the people in your group to find their skills and limits.

When scripting your ceremony, avoid open-ended cues. As Magenta Griffiths of Prodea Temple puts it:

> When planning a large ritual, never have a time when everyone says something without some check on what is said. Don't have as part of the ritual [the cue to], "tell your story." Some people will be too shy to say anything, and some will want to talk for an hour. Instead, have people "say your name and three words that describe you." Most people can say that much, and the person looking for an outlet will have to look elsewhere.[59]

Open-ended cues can also lead to individuals taking your ritual off in directions you never intended, and may not like. I've seen a number of liturgies ruined this way, both accidentally and deliberately. Remember, there's a thin line between empowering the participants and letting some destroy what others have worked hard to achieve.

Aesthetic, Psychological, and Cultural Themes

Thematic elements should suit the congregation and clergy available, as well as the occasion at hand. Every decision you make about the most beautiful way to do any given part of the liturgy is an aesthetic choice: formality, vocal mode, physical activity, dramatic approaches, unobtrusive cuing, site selection, costumes and props, music, etc. It's best to make each of these factors reinforce the others to produce a coherent whole. This in turn supports the unity of the group mind and its ability to focus the patterns of mana involved.

Your choice of psychological theme(s) can help greatly here. Is this to be a sad, silly, or solemn liturgy? Are you dealing with a birth

---

§ See all of Chapter 10.

that adds a member to your community, or a death that transforms it? What is the emotional relationship between the members of the group and the spirits or divinities to be contacted? Is the ceremony a celebration of a Holy Day—if so, what meanings does that Holy Day have for those participating? Knowing the answers to these questions adds tremendous power.

Another way to improve the unity and focus of your group is to design your liturgy around specific cultural themes. A Celtic liturgy is very different from a Native American or a Chinese liturgy. Every culture has symbols, styles, and metaphors that reinforce each other. Using these, and excluding ones from cultures that aren't congruent, gives your ritual a definite assist.

For example, try having your people dress in Slavic costumes, sing Slavic tunes, invoke Slavic deities in a Slavic language, and even drink Slavic liquor in your liturgy. The amount of Slavic-flavored mana raised will be tremendous, and the group mind will be a hundred times more unified and focused than the participants may be used to. It's possible to blend in cultural themes from related cultures (such as the Balts or the Norse, in this example) without too much damage. If a culture is too far removed (say East African, Japanese, or Inca), the clash of cultural symbols, signs, and metaphors may easily destroy the mana patterns your liturgy is supposed to create.

Which requires me to say a word or two about the mixing of Native American elements into Neopagan and New Age ceremonies. There's been a lot of that ever since shamanism became a fad in the New Age and Neopagan communities. Most of this mixing has been not only magically sloppy, but insulting to both the European and the Native American deities invoked. People have been taking deities, symbols, music, chants, and fragments of rituals from a dozen different Native American cultures and injecting these clumsily into Wiccan or New Age ceremonies. This has also been done recently with elements of Afro-American Mesopagan faiths by well-meaning but grossly ignorant Neopagans.

An argument can be made, however, that by adopting the ritual customs of previously despised minorities, Neopagans and New Agers are using the social-normative aspects of liturgy to make a conscious commitment to lessening racism and creedism in Western culture. This politically correct effort to express solidarity with oppressed peoples is also the morally correct thing to do, so it should be done well if it is to be done at all.

For twenty years, a man named Sun Bear mixed Native-American beliefs from several tribes, Western astrology, Wiccan rituals, and New-Age crystal consciousness into a new religion. I've participated in ceremonies based on his work, and they were beautiful and emotionally uplifting, but I don't think they were as powerful as authentic traditional Native-American rituals used to be, partly because too many unrelated tribal belief systems were mixed, and partly because Neopagans and other New Agers, who were not raised to be familiar with Native American spiritual and liturgical patterns, were the ones doing them.

There is merit in another argument, that Euro-Americans are practicing our ceremonies on land that used to be inhabited by the Native Americans, and that therefore we ought to pay attention to the local nature spirits and deities who used to be worshipped here. I see nothing wrong with including local references in your liturgies, provided that you've done your homework. Don't make an offering to an Iroquois nature spirit in Texas, or a Sioux buffalo goddess in New Jersey, unless the members of your group have very strong psychic links to those tribes. After all, one prime characteristic of polytheistic religions is locality. Except for those few Paganisms that have become world religions (such as Hinduism or Voodoo), Pagan deities are *not* omnipresent.

Learn how to pronounce the spirit and deity names correctly; learn what their associated metaphysical systems were, and what their religious symbols meant. Then you can *very carefully* start to blend appropriate bits and pieces into your local liturgies. Just because Native Americanism is suddenly popular, don't assume that you can pull in all that Amerindian-flavored mana without attention to the details of what you're doing. And for Goddess' sake, find out what shamanism really is before you start calling your ceremonies "Shamanic."[60]

Alternately, you might decide to celebrate your African ancestry by researching and recreating the ceremonies that your ancestors performed. You would need to be aware that the vast majority of African-Americans are descended from a small number of tribes in West Africa, and that the religious patterns of Southern, Eastern, Northern, or Central Africa were (and are) dramatically different. The ancient Egyptians were indeed black Africans, but that doesn't mean that Isis, Horus, Thoth, and Ra will fit in aesthetically or magically with Chango, Ogun, or Legba.

Fortunately the West African faiths are still alive, both in their Paleo- to Mesopagan forms, influenced by Christianity and Islam in modern West Africa, and in the Mesopagan transformations (Santeria, Macumba, Voudoun, etc.) they experienced in the Americas (with Christian but not Islamic influences). Tribes that spoke languages related to Yoruba would have had similar polytheologies, and therefore liturgical elements from their religions would blend reasonably well with each other.[61]

Part of the experimentation that Neopagans are now performing is to discover how far apart two cultures can be before they clash, instead of reinforcing each other, in a ritual. So far it seems that the various Celtic cultures work well together, as do the Norse and German, the Slavic and Baltic, and the Greek and Roman. But will mixing Baltic and Roman, or Celtic and Greek themes together in one rite ruin it? Or will all the cultural members of the Indo-European language family, or those within other language families, work together? Only time will tell.

Liturgical Languages

Some religious ceremonies use one or more foreign languages. Many people wonder why a ritual should be partly or even completely in a language other than the one people usually use in their day-to-day lives. There are actually several reasons why having a special language that is used in rituals can be a good idea.

To begin with, in the field of linguistics, the "Sapir-Whorf Hypothesis" states, roughly, that the language in which you think influences the types of thoughts you are capable of thinking easily. There are certain concepts in Tibetan, for example, that are extremely difficult to express in English, and vice versa.

Those of us who have tried the experiment have found that if you invoke a Celtic deity, for example, in a Celtic language, *you get answered!* Even with my badly pronounced, childish grasp of Modern Irish, I have been able to perform ceremonies, both publicly and in private, where the amount of mana raised was far beyond anything I have ever been able to do with Irish deities while speaking only English.

This is because of the magical Law of Similarity—by using Irish I am making myself more similar to the minds of the people who created/discovered the old gods and goddesses of Ireland (see RM and RE). In any event, I have heard the same story from people invoking Norse deities in Icelandic, Roman deities in Latin, Vedic ones in Sanskrit, Chinese ones in Chinese, West African ones in Yoruba, etc.

Using a nonordinary language also sends a clear message to the subconscious minds of the participants that something special is going on—after all, you're using magical words. These could be utter nonsense and they would still have the potential for powerful psychological (and therefore magical) effects, based on their sounds, volume, speed, etc. Think of the words we babble to our children, pets, or lovers in baby talk or the power of an incoherent scream of rage. If you use the same magical language on multiple occasions you will also reap the benefit of familiarity transforming those words into cues.[62]

I've encouraged people in the Neopagan community for years to use the ancient tongues in their rites. If you decide to do so in your liturgical designs, you may want to have the ceremonies be bilingual, with alternating English and non-English parts.

Here is an Irish example from a Neopagan Druid ceremony:

> ***Druid 1:*** Spirits of the old times and of this place, hallow these waters.
>
> ***Druid 2:*** *A sprideanna na seanaimsire agus na háite seo, beannaígí na h-uisci seo dúinn.*
>
> ***Druid 1:*** Share with us renewal of the Earth. Share with us comfort, knowledge, and blessing.
>
> ***Druid 2:*** *Roinnigí orainn athbheochan na Talún. Roinnigí oriann suaimhneas, eolas, agus beannacht.*
>
> ***Druid 1:*** Speak to our hearts, that we may become one with you all.
>
> ***Druid 2:*** *Labhraígí linn inár gcroí, le go mbeadh muid in aon bhall libse.*[63]

This style of bilingualism ensures that all the participants who do not speak the ceremonial language nonetheless understand what is being said. It also creates a "call and response" rhythm that can be very effective in generating and focusing mana.¶

Another way in which a foreign language can be integrated into a ritual smoothly is to use English litanies with repeating foreign responses, such as:

> **Lady of the Shining Moon, bless us!**
>
> *Benedicta nobis!*
>
> **Silver Huntress of the Night...**
>
> *Benedicta nobis!*
>
> **Dark Lady of the Mysteries...**
>
> *Benedicta nobis!*

You can also use a foreign language for ritual exclamations such as "So be it," "We are blessed," or "This is truth," etc. Once the members of your congregation have heard a phrase used a few times, they

---

¶ See Chapter 9, Raising and Focusing Mana.

should be able to repeat it on cue, and such phrases can be taught to newcomers during the preritual briefing (discussed in Chapter 11).

Your decisions about foreign languages, like those about cultural themes, will usually be based on the interests of the people you are creating the ceremonies for (and an accurate assessment about how committed they are). Use the language(s) and culture(s) for which they have the most affinity to guide you here.

8

How, Musical

Music and poetry are two of the most important arts for religious rituals. Melodies, songs, chants, and recitations not only generate emotional responses in the participants, and thus increase the mana in the circle, but they also focus that mana both polytheologically (by reinforcing shared beliefs) and magically (by creating the shared images within which the group's mana will flow and be shaped). Many problems with your liturgy's dramatic pacing are avoidable and/or solvable by musical means.

Bards have been respected and feared figures almost everywhere in the world, because people knew how magically powerful the songs of someone who understood magic could be. Bards, like anyone else who worked heavily with words, were considered masters of the Law of Words of Power, and their musical instruments made them even more capable of guiding both the minds of their listeners and the hidden forces of the cosmos. This is why your music director, choir leader, or bard needs to be part of your planning from the beginning, along with as many of the musicians as possible.

Even if the members of a given group think they are all tone deaf, or can't carry a tune in a bucket, they should still try to use music and poetry whenever they can and might wish to try "plain chant," which is often easier to sing than fully melodic songs are.

In this chapter, I'll present a few examples of how sung or rhymically recited words can be effectively used in ritual.

Since the vast majority of Neopagan congregations are of mixed genders, these examples will assume that situation. However, they can and should be rewritten to meet a group's needs. [I'm using mostly my own compositions here, not because I think that they are superior, but because I know where all the copyright credits belong—often a problem with popular Neopagan chants.]

POETRY

Aidan Kelly, a founder of the New Reformed Orthodox Order of the Golden Dawn, a major tradition/denomination of Wicca, explained the ritual power of poetry very clearly back in 1975. Speaking of "the Lady," who is the goddess worshipped by Wiccans, and identifying (or at least associating) her with the Jungian collective unconscious as distinct from a person's individual conscious mind ("the I-mind"), he said:

> The function of symbolism and of symbolic language in a ritual is to open up a channel of communication with the Goddess… When the Lady deigns to speak to the I-mind, she does so in symbols, which the I-mind must learn to interpret in order to get any good from them. Conversely, if the I-mind wants to speak to the Lady, it must speak in her language or else go unheard, for the Lady apparently couldn't care less about the I-mind's ordinary reasons for wanting something …

> Poetry, being [an] emotionally charged language that operates on many levels of meaning at once, can arouse the interest of the Lady and open up the channel of communication with her, whereas ordinary, prosaic speech has no such effect …

> By "poetry" here, I mean not the highly intellectual art of modern poetry, but simple English verse. If you've never had any formal training in verse craft, try studying *The Annotated Moth-*

er Goose and traditional English ballads; with a little practice in such forms, you should soon get the hang of constructing verses that rhyme, scan, and say what you want them to.[64]

IMPROVING YOUR CHANTS

Properly done chanting can raise a *lot* of mana. My wife Phaedra has some useful tips here, from a paper she wrote on ritual chanting in 1992. After discussing the importance of choosing chants and songs with appropriate words[*] and rhythms related to the goal and target of a ritual, as well as the specific altered state of consciousness to be created, she continues:

> Considering content is not enough. How are the words spoken? What are the sounds? Explosive consonants (like K or F or P) are going to create a different feeling than S or W or R. Vowel sounds are basic to toning…[†]

> How complex are the words? If we are really heading to a fever pitch, it will be hard to stay verbal. Remembering a two-verse chant will become impossible—and trying to do so will inhibit accessing the ecstatic state. A power chant will often be either quite short, say two lines, or contain a lot of repetition. Some examples: "Fire flow free/fire flow through me" (note the Fs); "We are the old people/we are the new people/we are the same people/stronger than before."

---

[*] I've lost count of the number of times the Pagan Top Ten chant of "We all come from the Goddess and to her we shall return, like a drop of rain flowing to the ocean" has caused rain to begin falling on the chanters and their festival or parade…

[†] Toning is the singing of single sounds like "ah" or "oh." It can blur into chanting as such when simple words are sung as separate phonemes, such as *Aum:* "ah…oo…m…"

It is often effective to shorten the chant as you go along in order to increase the intensity. For example, "Fire flow free/ fire flow through me" becomes "Fire flow free/fire flow free" becomes "Fire!/Fire!/Fire!"‡ The chant that starts out with, "We are the old people..." simplifies to "Stronger than before" and then just "Stronger! Stronger! Stronger!" Both can, of course, go further by dissolving into the ever popular (and power-effective) yells and yelps. [65]

While I personally enjoy howling at the moon, the yelling and yelping she mentions is not usually appropriate for other than a single-peak masculine spell-casting (see Chapter 9), and then only sometimes.

When songs or chants are performed in ways to accentuate the physical vibrations caused in the performers or listeners, or musical instruments (such as drums or gongs) are used to physically shake the listeners, these auditory techniques blend into kinesthetic ones such as dancing (see Chapter 9).

One common method of using chants is to start out softly, then gradually build up the volume and speed of both the voices and the music (especially drums). Decide on a cue—such as the bard(s) raising their arms halfway up—to indicate that the last verse is coming. This part gets tricky. You can't just stop the music abruptly at the end, since folks are likely to start yelling and screaming (especially at a large festival rite), and your carefully woven web of energies will go splattering in all directions. If the musicians and chant facilitators just drop their volume on cue and slow down for the final verse, with no visible signal to the rest of the grove, then the other participants may not notice, but instead continue to increase the volume and the speed of their chanting until it all falls apart.

Try this in a circular sacred space: at the proper moment, have your chant facilitators or junior bards (whom you have carefully placed equidistant around the circle) step three paces toward the

---

‡ Which should not be shouted in a crowded temple...

center, turn around with their arms held high, face the congregation and gradually lower their arms as they lower and slow their voices, while the musicians lower and slow the music. The senior bard can be doing the same gesture near the main altar, slowly rotating in her/his place. The chant will end with everyone slowly whispering it, then stopping simultaneously. The chant facilitators can then return to their previous positions, and the energies in the grove will be at a strong and steady peak. Or you can have the chant facilitators raise their arms to raise the volume and tempo of the chanting into a crescendo, if that's what you need at that point in the rite.

In a rectangular sacred space where the altar or other visual focus is towards the front, the bard(s) can use the same methods by stepping between the altar and the congregation. These techniques will work even better if they have been used a few times earlier in the rite, or at previous ceremonies.

Readers who have attended Neopagan rituals, especially at large festivals, will have noticed that many of them make frequent use of what I call...

The Generic Pagan Chant

(© 1993, 2001 words & music by IB — and 10,000 Pagans)[66]

A-minor, D-minor, A-minor, D-minor.
    This is another Pagan chant.
You can tell that it's real old
    'cause it sounds just like a funeral dirge.
A-minor, D-minor, A-minor, D-minor,
    A-minor, D-minor, A-Flaaaat!

Too many people in the early decades of Wicca apparently decided that all our songs and chants had to be in minor keys, either to make us sound more religious to hostile outsiders, or because they assumed all British Isles folk music was that way. Of course, why they thought that Greek, Roman, Egyptian, Slavic, etc., gods and goddesses would enjoy British folk music is beyond me.

The irony is that our supposed revival of a peasant religion should have had such upper-class biases against the rowdy sorts of music that members of peasant cultures usually enjoy. So please—unless you are at a funeral for someone (and maybe not even then), use music that is lively and happy. Try modal settings for your instruments, or at least major keys!

CALL AND RESPONSE

"Call and response" is a technique familiar to anyone who has attended an African-American church ceremony, or a Vodoun or Santería one (the source of all three can be found in West African Paleopaganism). It can be thought of as formalized conversation, usually between the leaders of a ritual and the other participants, in which they mutually reinforce their beliefs and intentions. Here's an example of how call and response can be used at the beginning of a ritual:

Opening Chant

(© 1989, 2001 words & music by IB)

Priestess:	Sisters, tell us why we're here?
Women:	We're here to worship the Goddess.
Priest:	Brothers, tell us why we're here?
Men:	We're here to worship the God.
Priestess:	We're here to worship our Lady dear,
	Who gives us courage to face all fear,
	Who brings us hope and love and cheer.
	We're here to worship the Goddess!
Priest:	We're here to worship the Horn-éd Man,
	Who gives us wisdom to understand,
	Who brings us strength for heart and hand.
	We're here to worship the God!
Priestess:	Tell me sisters, why we're here?
Women:	We're here to worship the Goddess!

Priest:	Tell me brothers, why we're here?
Men:	We're here to worship the God!

This fully serves the liturgical purpose of announcing that the ceremony is beginning and why the people have gathered (to be reinforced a few steps later). Whether sung or chanted, it should be done liltingly—not droned—so the internal rhythm can get the ritual off to a spritely (so to speak) start.

Note the accented "e" in the third verse; it's there to remind the HP to pronounce "Horn-éd" as two syllables, in order to maintain the rhythm.

Symmetry can be important in providing magical closure, so at the end of the ritual there should be a similar...

Closing Chant

(© 1989, 2001 words & music by IB)

Priestess:	Tell me brothers, what we have done.
Men:	We have worshipped the Goddess!
Priest:	Tell me sisters, what we have done.
Women:	We have worshipped the God!
Priestess:	We have been blessed with holy grace.
Priest:	Return we now to time and space.
Priestess:	The circle fades without a trace.
All:	Our worship now is done!

The beginning recalls the first four lines of the *Opening Chant,* altered for final reinforcement and affirming that both mortal genders have honored both divine genders.

Musical Instruments and Styles

Almost any musical instrument or style can be used effectively in a liturgy, though you will want to pay close attention to the aesthetic and cultural factors involved. Because most Neopagan groups don't own real estate, and therefore tend to have temporary sacred spaces, especially ones out in the woods or down upon beaches, the most common musical instruments in Neopagan liturgies are highly portable ones such as drums, rattles, flutes, guitars, etc. Other liberal religious traditions may have church buildings available, and thus be able to incorporate pianos, organs, or harpsichords into their rituals, as well as larger numbers of medium-sized instruments.

Drums have become increasingly popular ritual tools in recent years, especially in Neopagan and New Age liturgies, because of their ability to create *entrainment* of the heartbeats (and thus the mana) of the participants to the rhythms played. Also, because Western culture thinks of drums as primitive instruments that are therefore easy to play, many folks who would hesitate to try using a violin or a saxophone will attempt playing a drum. This is not always a good thing, as badly played drums can mess up a ceremony as quickly as any other abused instrument. Still, simple rhythms played on inexpensive drums, rattles, shakers, and tambourines can add a powerful effect to a ritual and are well worth experimenting with.

While I love drums, I *don't* recommend that drummers at Wiccan or other Neopagan rituals use authentic Santeria or Voudoun drum rhythms *unless they know exactly what they are doing!* The African deities *will* come when you call them, and they expect to be treated correctly according to *their* traditions — not yours!

I strongly recommend getting some books and video recordings on basic drum techniques (or attending local open drum circles) and learning to use whatever drums you own as effectively as possible. Remember that most drums are meant to be group, not solo, instruments, and that they have rules and traditions for getting the most out of them.

Liturgical music does not *have* to be pre-modern or stereotypically folksy. I have heard and enjoyed rock and roll, classical, and jazz in Neopagan rituals (punk, heavy metal, and clash music didn't seem to work as well, but maybe that's just me). For Druidic rituals, Celtic music (both ancient and modern) is always appropriate. For Asatruar ones, German or Scandinavian music works best, and so forth.

Feel free to use modern technology in your rituals. I have done rituals in situations where microphones and a sound system were both available and necessary. They worked just fine, though we did have to be careful to not trip over the cords. Using remote head-phones/mics will solve that particular problem, though you might want to disguise them as part of your ceremonial costumes.

If you can't get live musicians, use recorded music through the best sound system you can manage. This will require your rehearsals to use the same recordings, so that everyone learns how to match the timing of the tapes, CDs, or iPods. You will want to have one person whose job it is to start and stop the music at the right times, and who knows enough to pay attention to any pacing difficulties (or signals sent by one of the clergy). But don't bother trying to record the results of drawings-down (possessions)—the deities seem to enjoy making that difficult.

Repetition and Refrain

The more the words, rhythm, and melody of one part of your ritual relate to similar aspects of other parts, the easier it is to create, maintain, and direct the group mind of the participants. Wiccan ritual is ideally suited to demonstrate this principle.

Wiccan cosmology sees the four elements of Earth, Air, Fire, and Water as basic to all existence (a fifth element, Spirit, links them together). The four Elements are symmetrical, being four possible combinations of hot and cold, dry and wet, and repeated symmetrical references to them can easily be used to reinforce that cosmology in the magical space being created/recognized. Here's a song/chant to bless the four elemental tools that will be used to bless and exorcise the circle:

Elemental Tool Blessing

(© 1989, 2001 words & music by IB)

[Priestess blesses incense]

Priestess: We bless thee, oh creature of air,
            That thou mayest purify all;
            Freeing us here from all care,
            As on your bright wisdom we call.

All: So mote it be!

[Priestess blesses charcoal/flame]

Priestess: We bless thee, oh creature of fire,
             That thou mayest purify all;
             Igniting our holy desire,
             As on your fierce courage we call.

All: So mote it be!

[Priest blesses water]

Priest: We bless thee, oh creature of water,
             That thou mayest purify all;
             Cleansing each son and each daughter,
             As on your deep feelings we call.

All: So mote it be!

[Priest blesses salt/soil]

Priest: We bless thee, oh creature of earth,
             That thou mayest purify all;
             Renewing all that of true worth,
             As on your strong power we call.

All: So mote it be!

Notice how each verse repeats the form and many of the words of the preceding ones, with modifications appropriate to the element concerned. This helps make the words easier to memorize for the speakers, reinforces what they have learned in religious classes, and connects them later in the rite with the elemental attributions of the spirits associated with the Four Quarters.

The refrain at the end of each verse, "So mote it be," is a phrase borrowed from Freemasonry, where it essentially means "Amen" or "So be it."[§] The use of a refrain that all can join also helps the members of the group avoid slipping into an experience of themselves as "audience" and "performers." While this is a minor problem in the

---

§ There used to be an organized movement within Wicca to insist on saying the more modern English version in a Russian style, but the so-be-it union fell apart in 1991…

average Wiccan coven of three to five members, it becomes a major issue in doing larger group rituals at holidays and festivals.

When creating the Wiccan magical circle, Spirit can be seen to be present in the center of two crossing lines (North-South and East-West) that link opposite Elements associated with the cardinal directions. Using that idea, here's another example of how repeating patterns can reinforce earlier ones, in a *Quarter Calling*:

Quarter Calling

(© 1990, 2001 words by IB, music by unknown S.C.A. bard.)

> *[East]*
>
> *Winged One, Spirit of Air,*
> > *your children invite you here.*
>
> *Come on the winds of the sunrise,*
> > *give us your vision so clear.*
>
> *You are the gentle spring breezes,*
> > *you are the glory of flight.*
>
> *Winged One, Spirit of Air,*
> > *keep us wise through our rite.*
>
> *[South]*
>
> *Fierce One, Spirit of Fire,*
> > *your children invite you here.*
>
> *Come with your blazing noon passion,*
> > *banish all sorrow and fear.*
>
> *You are the flickering candle,*
> > *you are the bonfire bright.*
>
> *Fierce One, Spirit of Fire,*
> > *keep us brave through our rite.*
>
> *[West]*
>
> *Swift One, Spirit of Water,*
> > *your children invite you here.*

Come on the waves of the sunset,

        bring to us joy and good cheer.

You are the well of deep comfort,

        you are the crashing waves height.

Swift One, Spirit of Water,

        keep us sure through our rite.

[North]

Hoofed One, Spirit of Earth,

        your children invite you here.

Come from the mountains of midnight,

        with new strength and vigor appear.

You are the field of our pleasure,

        you are the source of our might.

Hoofed One, Spirit of Earth,

        keep us strong through our rite.

[Center]

Winged One...

Fierce One...

Swift One...

Hoofed One...

        Keep us pure through our rite.

These words can be sung or chanted by the Priestess, the Priest, four volunteers, or whoever else wishes. Also, in any circle larger than nine feet across, have the callers stand at the opposite sides from the directions to which they are calling. That way, everyone in the circle will be likely to actually hear them! The pattern here is a little more complex than that in the *Elemental Tool Blessing:*

{Animal adjective} One, Spirit of {Element}

        your children invite you here.

Come {elemental metaphor} {time of day},

        {With elemental gift/resource}.

You are the {gentle aspect },
>you are the {frightening aspect}
{Animal adjective} One, Spirit of {Element}
>keep us {elemental virtue} through our rite.

Matching the *Quarter Calling* near the beginning of the rite is naturally a *Quarter Farewell* near the end:

Quarter Farewell

(© 1991, 2001 words by Deborah Lipp, music by IB.)

[East]	*Wise One...*
[South]	*Brave One...*
[West]	*Sure One...*
[North]	*Strong One...*
[Center]	*We bid you now hail and farewell.*
	Go by the powers that brought you,
	Go by the unweaving spell.
	As thy bright pentagrams fade,
	Depart, 'ere the circle is gone.
[East]	*Winged One...*
[South]	*Fierce One...*
[West]	*Swift One...*
[North]	*Hoofed One...*
[Center]	*As we say, be it done!*

As is usually the case with songs and chants near the end of a
ritual, this matching bit is shorter and less ornate. Notice how the
elemental virtues are mentioned first and the animal adjectives are
used last, thus reversing the original order of terms.

Notice also that this *Quarter Farewell* doesn't use the all-too-common
phrase, "Go if you must, stay if you will," that (far too) many Wiccans
have added to their liturgies in recent years. At the Celtic feast of *Sam-
hain* (known to moderns as Halloween), the Gates Between the Worlds

may usually be left open safely until dawn. On all other occasions, it's best to assume that the spirits of the Quarters (especially if they are deities!) have other things to do than hang around and party, and that a ritual's artistic, psychic, and spiritual closure requires their departure.

Teaching Songs

One of the many purposes for which songs and chants are used is for teaching and reinforcing a group's beliefs and practices. Songs about a particular deity tell everyone present what they believe about that deity and can be effectively used as descriptive invocations in phases two and three of your liturgy. Here, for example, is a song designed to invoke the presence of the Dagda, the omnifunctional All-Father of the ancient Irish people, in a Neopagan Druid ritual:

A Hymn to the Dagda

(© 1993, 1999 by Isaac Bonewits, music Irish trad. "Ta Na La")

Hear us Dag- / da, All Father
Answer us / O Supreme Knower
Sing now the poets / to praise your name
Return again / unto your people.

Éist a Dhag- / da, Ollathair
Freagairt orainn / a Ruad Rofheasa
Canann anois filí / chun do ainm molann
Tar ais arís / chugainn do chlann.

You are the flame / that burns within
The royal hearth, / or an outcast's hovel;
The sacrifi- / cial fire as well,
The giver and / the gift that's given.
You are the heat / of a warrior bold
When fighting for / the tribe's survival;
The firey pas- / sion of our loins,
The holy spark / of live renewing.

Éist a Dhag- / da, Ollathair
Freagairt orainn / a Ruad Rofheasa
Canann anois filí / chun do ainm molann
Tar ais arís / chugainn do chlann.

A royal scep- / ter is your club,
A druid's wand / to wield your power;
A weapon strong, / Outsiders' bane,
A phallus proud, / to please the Ladies.
We praise you for / your mighty mirth,
As you roar in- / to bed or battle;
Your harp that plays / the seasons round,
Your cauldron filled / with gifts unending.

Éist a Dhag- / da, Ollathair
Freagairt orainn / a Ruad Rofheasa
Canann anois filí / chun do ainm molann
Tar ais arís / chugainn do chlann.

The people call / you once again
From many tribes / we give you honor.
Earth Mother needs / your potent joy,
Burn bright within / us, God of Fire!

Éist a Dhag- / da, Ollathair
Freagairt orainn / a Ruad Rofheasa
Canann anois filí / chun do ainm molann
Tar ais arís / chugainn do chlann.

The Irish words are a translation of the opening verse and are re-
peated to take advantage of the power of using a liturgical language.
Other examples of this bilingual technique can be found in *A Hymn to
Bridget* and *A Hymn to the Morrigan* (see *BEGD*).

Here's another example, this one to teach about some Celtic
goddesses:

There Were Three Sisters

(© 1987, 1999, words by Isaac Bonewits, music English trad.
"Henry Martin")

> There were three sisters in our ancient land,
> In our ancient land there were three.
> And they did dispute which of them
> Should be, should be, should be,
> Greatest of all in the hearts of the free.
>
> Oh, first spoke Danu, the Mother of All,
> Her voice was as rich as the earth:
> "I give them my cattle, my grain,
> And mirth, and mirth, and mirth.
> Freedom without joy is of little worth."
>
> And then spoke Macha, the Goddess of War,
> Her voice was the roar of the wave:
> "I give but courage, for fear will
> Enslave, enslave, enslave.
> Freedom's a gift given but to the brave."
>
> Now third spoke Rian, the Light of the Moon,
> Her voice was as vast as the sky:
> "I give to their thoughts great wings
> To fly, to fly, to fly.
> Freedom means naught if you never ask why."

[Repeat first verse. Instrumental break.]

> But then came Bridget, the Queen of All Arts,
> Her voice was a flickering flame:
> "My sisters I fear your gifts miss
> Their aim, their aim, their aim.
> None but through me can their true freedom claim."
>
> "For pleasure and riches are fleeting at best,
> And a warrior's strength is quite brief.

And knowledge alone brings them naught
Save grief, save grief, save grief.
Without beauty's fire within their belief."

"My healers restore hope to those who despair.
My smiths forge them weapons so grand.
My bards cause all those who kneel
To stand, to stand, to stand.
The fires of Freedom are lit by my hand!"

There were four Sisters in our ancient land...

To sum up, if you want your liturgies to be as powerful and focused as possible, use the chants, music, and technology that will inspire and unify the participants, while teaching them what you want them to know and do, and matching the aesthetics of the rituals concerned.

9
How, Magical

Religious Magic and Magical Religions

Magical techniques are used in every religion, though western religions won't usually admit it. Yet any anthropologist or polytheologian can see Jewish, Christian, and Islamic rituals as magical and/or psychological ceremonies being done with pre-defined spiritual goals. Those that aren't pure worship liturgies or individual prayers are usually rites of passage or rites of intensification.

Every Christian sacrament, for example, has its counterparts in most other religions. Baptism is to put up *psychic shields* (fields of mana designed to keep out or filter other mana) and, for adults, to also cut their psychic links with other divinities and spiritual systems. Confirmation (like a Bar or Bas Mitzvah) is a standard coming-of-age rite, removing some of those childhood psychic shields and making the recipients at least partially responsible for their own protection, as well as integrating them into the adult psychic network of the tribe.

A conscientious clergyperson will see no conflict in using the best art and music that his/her culture has to offer, in order to make the rituals of their religion as effective as possible. In the same way, he or she also owes it to their congregation to use sound magical principles in designing, preparing, and performing worship rituals for them.

Scholars of what they call "new religious movements" (even though many are merely new to the West) have coined the term *magical religions* to refer to religions in which average members are expected and encouraged to develop their own magical skills and to use these in their religious activities. Almost all of the Neopagan religions, many of the Mesopagan ones, and almost all Paleopagan faiths would count as magical religions by this definition, as would more than a few modern liberal religious movements from New Thought and Christian Science to the latest New Age faith.

As Driver puts it...

> While Frazer, Bateson, and many other writers try to defend religion by denigrating magic, Van Gennep's position, holding magic and religion together, is better. We may say that some forms of magic and magical belief are less intelligent than others, remembering that the magico-religious, as Van Gennep called it, has crass as well as admirable examples; but without magic, religion is powerless. Since the rites of religion are techniques of transformation, Van Gennep realized, when people divorce religion from magic they end up with metaphysics on the one hand, empirical science on the other, and religion gone. This is the fate to which much liberal religion in Western society has very nearly come. Having mostly turned away from its own magic, it has little to offer, and its numbers are declining.[67]

So let's discuss the magical aspects of religious rituals in a straightforward, polytheological manner, instead of just beating around the (burning?) bush.

Targets and Goals

If you are planning a garden, then your goal is to produce food, and your target may be either a particular chunk of ground in the backyard or a window box in your kitchen. Either way, if you don't plant your seeds into real, specific ground somewhere, you aren't going to wind up with many tomatoes.

If you're a surgeon dealing with a person who has lung cancer, your goal will be to heal that person and your target will be the specific tumors that have to be removed. Doing an easier procedure instead (such as taking out her appendix) won't suffice, even if so doing constitutes a successful operation.

If you're a technological rainmaker hired by some farmers to end a drought, your goal will be to cause the needed amount of rain to fall over a specific area, without causing meteorological side effects hundreds of miles away. Your target might be a specific cloudbank, at a particular altitude, over a certain location. If you don't deliver exactly the right amount of chemicals to exactly the right spot, at exactly the right time, you will probably not get the results you wanted, no matter how much fun you had trying.

It should be clear at this point: the *goal* is the final result you are after, the *target* is the precise person(s), place(s) and/or thing(s) you need to affect in order to achieve your goal. This is one of the great unwritten secrets of magic. If you want your liturgy to have any positive results other than personal pleasure, an energy buzz, or a boost to your ego, you *must* pay attention to this in your planning.

Each of the examples given above has parallels in the realm of ritual. Agricultural magic, psychic healing, and weather working all require that you focus your mana upon a specific target in order to achieve a specific goal. If you haven't clearly defined your goal, nor specified your target, nor designed the ritual to guide your mana towards that target, the odds are very high that little of use is going to occur—and some very *unuseful* results may happen instead.

If you want to make the crops grow better, pick a specific hunk of dirt with plants in it, then focus on those plants and that dirt. If you want to heal Aunt Matilda's lung cancer, send the mana into her lungs. If you want to make it rain, choose your cloud. *Don't* just send vaguely fertile, healthy, or rainy thoughts out in all directions with the assumption that "the power will go where it's needed." [68] Trust me, it won't.

As we discussed earlier, rituals being done for practical physical purposes, such as starting or stopping rain, healing sick people, etc., are thaumaturgical. Rituals being done for impractical spiritual purposes, such as attaining enlightenment, strengthening the Gods, or honoring the ancestors are theurgical (as are those done for psychotherapeutic purposes, such as self-empowerment ceremonies). Like most pairs of terms in polytheology, these are not opposites in the dualistic "must be black or must be white" sense, but the extremes at either end of a continuum. *Most thaumaturgical rituals contain theurgical elements and vice versa.* Nonetheless, this distinction must be clearly spelled out when designing a ritual.

The mental clarity needed to define a goal and to select a target which, if affected properly, is likely to achieve or manifest that goal, is just as important when designing theurgical rituals as it is with thaumaturgical ones. If your goal is personal spiritual growth, then your target is yourself and the other people participating in the rite. If your goal is the ethical enlightenment of the whaling industry, then your target might be the specific individuals who make the decisions to kill whales. This would require you to find out their names, appearances, and locations. If your goal is to honor and strengthen ancestors, nature spirits or the Gods, then they are the targets—and you should pick one or two of them by name and appearance!

From a polytheological point of view, the primary distinction between magical and religious rituals as such, is that in religious ones you can afford to have secondary goals, each with its own target. This works better if the secondary goals are theurgical ones, whether the primary goal is theurgical or thaumaturgical. Also, in religious rituals, you can ask the Gods to help you select the correct target(s) through divination, and/or to provide necessary fine-tuning of the mana, and/or to provide any needed ethical screening (escape clauses) for your target(s).

Since 80–85 percent of the people in the world use vision as their primary sensing mode, the process called *visualization* is the one most often used to keep a group's attention focused on a goal and target. This requires every person in a group to create and maintain a more-

or-less identical mental image of the goal and the target, with the target taking center stage. The closer each person's images are to those being used by the others, then the higher the probability is that the mana sent toward the target will be effective. But if every person in a group has a different mental image of the goal and/or the target, then even the most powerful of ceremonies will be a wasted effort. This is why there is so much emphasis on focus and unity in liturgical design. To put it another way: *fuzzy rituals get fuzzy results.*

Remember that you need to visualize both the goal you want to achieve, and the target you wish to affect, in a future tense—*as you wish them to be.* Putting more mana into the status quo will only make things more the way they already are, not change them in any useful fashion.

You will also need to consider variables in the target, such as the amount and type of change needed (inertia), whether any sort of magical shielding or psychic interference will be present, the complexity of the changes intended (the information content of your spell), etc.[69]

Raising and Focusing Mana

There are many different ways to *raise* or stimulate the generation of mana for magical and/or religious use, and then to shape or *focus* it. Each method has its particular strengths and weaknesses, will appeal to different people at different times, and will be appropriate or inappropriate for use in particular circumstances. Some simply won't work well in liturgies at all.

Before we look at some of these methods, however, Phaedra has more wisdom to share with us:

> Do not confuse *feeling* energy with raising or controlling energy. Raising energy is just that—raising or increasing it. So many people confuse any energy with effective energy, any state [of consciousness] change with an appropriate state change.[70]

All too often I have had people tell me how wonderful a ritual was and how much energy they had felt during it, when the ritual itself was disorganized, unfocused, and had raised little or no useful mana at all. Why would participants in such rites be happy then? Because most rituals, no matter how badly designed or performed, *stimulate the production of endorphins*, brain chemicals that suppress pain and make people feel good. Like the similar chemical morphine, endorphins can become addictive, leading people to want to repeat the activities they found pleasurable. This may be yet another reason why magical and religious rituals are found in every human culture—we evolved to find them a source of pleasure.

While you should enjoy practicing the liturgical and magical arts, just having fun doing a ritual is usually not enough to consider it an effective or useful ceremony.* You need to be paying attention to both the quantity and the quality of the mana you are raising, as well as using appropriate techniques to focus and use the mana.

In the previous chapter, we looked at the use of music and poetry to raise and focus mana. Now let's look at some other methods of doing that effectively.

Meditation

Meditation, in the sense of calming and focusing the mind, is a truly ancient method of raising and focusing mana. While it usually takes a very long time to generate high amounts of mana, an experienced meditator can often pull in or *tap* significant quantities of mana from outside of his/her body in a short period.† Meditating congregants usually have more time in which to concentrate on a desired goal and target—to completely clarify the information content of the spell and then to give it multiple repetitions—than do those who must concentrate and create some sort of focus in brief periods.

Icons and Idolns

The use of two- or three-dimensional representations is an age-old method for stirring emotions (and thus of raising mana) as well as for

---

* Unless fun *was* the entire goal of the rite!

† See the tapping discussion below.

focusing attention. A drawing, painting, carving, sculpture, or photograph of a person, concept, or spirit can cause both the clergy and the congregation to experience very strong emotions, while giving them a clear image of a target or goal. Shamans and medicine people of all times and places have considered such visual stimuli as among their most valuable tools. Icons and idols usually absorb mana from both the worshippers and the entities depicted, as well as becoming ever more effective tapping tools (see below).

Dance

Men and women have always used dancing, as well as running, spinning, and other physical activities, as ways to go into altered states of consciousness and to release magical powers. There doesn't seem to be a single human culture in which dancing is not used for magical and religious purposes (not till this century anyway), with many of the procedures being incredibly complex and taking hours or days to complete.

Dancing can be quite effective at raising mana in a liturgy, provided those who are dancing actually know how to dance! As I have often said, holding hands and stumbling around in a circle is *not* dancing. Unless you are working with a small group of people, dancing is usually best left to specialists, for both aesthetic reasons and safety issues.‡ If some (or all) of your group wish to use dancing to raise mana, they should attend dance classes at a local folk dance club or medievalist organization long enough to learn a few basic principles. On the other paw, if the aesthetics of your liturgies are rock-and-rollish, then hanging out in nightclubs for a few weekends might be all they need!

Mana stimulates mana—the more you generate, the more you attract, and vice versa. Rhythmic sounds and actions can control these feedback loops, altering the strength and speed of the buildup, as well as focusing the consciousness of each participant. A concert is a good secular place to see such mana feedback loops. If the artists are truly talented, there is a palpable energy exchange between the

---

‡   See Chapter 5, Physical Challenges and Sensory Challenges.

audience and the performers. Expert performers learn to shape the feedback loops to produce the total artistic effect they want.

Mind-Altering Substances

Certain beverages and herbal potions can cause their users to generate enormous amounts of mana and/or open up their users to large inflows of mana, but are usually worthless for liturgical purposes. It is very hard to do fine-tuning while under the influence of strong mind-altering substances, because the pattern-forming aspects of the mind are usually distorted and confused by them. The perception of reality can shift so drastically that the potion-using clergyperson (such as a shaman, medicine person, etc.) may easily slide into what most observers—including members of her/his own tribe—would consider temporary or permanent insanity. While some drugs may work well in very small groups of trained users, they are usually a bad idea for rituals that may be attended by untrained members of the general public—not to mention the distracting effects of having your liturgy crashed by law enforcement agents!

The only socially acceptable, and therefore legal, drugs in the western world today are refined sugar, tobacco, caffeine, and alcohol, not all of which are suitable for use in public worship rituals,§ although the use of wine, beer, or ale is common.

Sex

Since anything that gets people excited will generate mana, sexual activities of all sorts have been used in religious and magical rituals for thousands of years. What we think of as sexual energy is one of the ways that mana manifests within humans and animals.

Sex magic, however, is not suitable for liturgical use, for many reasons. Safe, ethical, and effective use of sex as a mana source in a group requires that all the participants be mature, well-balanced, self-confident, and self-disciplined individuals who share the same erotic preferences, are willing to take directions, and who limit their

---

§ See Chapter 5's discussion of allergies in Physical Challenges.

sexual activities to within the group. How likely is it that the people who come to your liturgies will fit this profile?

Western culture is so schizophrenic about sexuality that any form of it being even suggested in a liturgy will offend many participants. If you have anyone under eighteen years old attending your ritual, just mentioning sex, let alone doing anything that looks sexual, may get you arrested. Despite the earthy sensuality of Neopagan beliefs and lifestyles, using sex to raise mana is something best kept behind closed doors among consenting adults for the next hundred years or so.

But sex and drugs and rock and roll aren't the only controversial ways of raising mana.

SACRIFICES

Among the commonest means of raising mana in religious rites are *sacrifices*. This word is highly charged with meanings, both positive and negative. To sacrifice something originally meant to make it holy, usually by giving it to a spirit. As a noun, it meant that which had been given. Even today the primary meaning is to give something to a higher¶ cause or greater purpose than continued personal use or enjoyment.

Neopagans don't fear our deities very much, so we don't usually do *propitiatory sacrifices*, which are the ones meant to gain divine favor when anger or indifference is expected. Since we don't pay much attention to demons or nasty spirits of any sort (except for an occasional exorcism), we certainly don't bother to give them *apotropaic sacrifices*, which are the kind that are meant to placate evil spirits in order to get them to turn aside their wrath.[71]

Thanksgiving sacrifices are simply a way of showing a spirit that his/her/its past blessings are appreciated. *Supportive sacrifices*[72] are offerings made to strengthen the spirit worshipped or to express one's love. Most Neopagan sacrifices are of these two sorts, given to the Goddesses and Gods out of love, as a way of thanking and strengthening them,

---

¶ The habit of referring to spirits as higher may owe something to mammalian status rituals that often involve displays of height.

and of showing our faith in them, as well as in hopes of persuading them to help us with our mortal problems.

From a magical point of view, the purpose of a sacrifice is to feed as much mana as possible to the entities being worshipped, in order to encourage a return flow of mana, which can then be used for thaumaturgical and/or theurgical purposes. Nonphysical sacrifices include the mana generated from abstinence and/or fasting, the keeping or breaking of food or other taboos, hard work, artistic creation, etc. Physical sacrifices have historically included plants, animals, and even people—all of which were sacrificed by our ancestors at one time or another. Why?

It's fairly obvious that the killing of a living being, even fruits and vegetables, is going to release a certain amount of mana,[73] which could then be shaped by the clergy and sent through the Gates Between the Worlds to the divine or other spirits being worshipped. Yet our ancestors also sacrificed inanimate objects—not just magically charged, ceremonial ones, but jewelry, weapons, even eating utensils. How could the destruction or throwing away (into rivers, wells, pits, etc.) of these nonliving objects release mana? The answer is that the act of sacrifice releases as much mana from the sacrificer (if not more than) as it does from the object sacrificed itself. If you had a valuable ring and you threw it into Niagara Falls** as a sacrifice to the god who dwells there, wouldn't you get a little emotional? If you took your best hunting bow and burned it as a sacrifice to Diana, the Huntress, don't you think you'd raise a significant amount of mana to give her?

When most people still raised their own food, sacrifices of crops and herds were partly this sort of financial sacrifice. They were also a practical source of nutrition, since the worshippers and/or the clergy often consumed the edible parts of the sacrifices. In ancient Greece, for example, the sacrificial feasts were an important part of people's social lives and often a way of feeding the poor.

** Be careful about putting items that might be toxic into running or standing water, however. Polluting the Earth Mother is likely to offend the deities rather than please them.

Every known Paleopagan culture practiced human sacrifice at some point in its early history. Almost all of them gave it up eventually, usually as a result of economic changes. Most cultures have a folktale in which the conversion from human sacrifice to animal or symbolic sacrifice is made. Most Mesopagan and all Neopagan groups absolutely forbid human sacrifice.

Many Neopagans believe that the goddesses and gods today are far more interested in receiving our sacrifices of time, energy, money, and other signs of commitment to saving the Earth Mother, than they are in receiving the sorts of sacrifices they used to get.

Blood sacrifices, in any event, are messy, difficult for most Westerners to do (unless they were raised on a farm) without excess pain to the animal, and simply unnecessary by Neopagan beliefs.[††] Additionally, most Neopagans and members of other liberal religions (especially the vegetarians and animal-rights activists) consider them morally repugnant, and far too reminiscent of Satanism and other forms of Christian dualism.

So including a blood sacrifice of any sort in a modern ceremony is far more likely to offend your congregation than it is to uplift them, not to mention getting you arrested.

As for human sacrifice, an accusation that is frequently thrown at minority religions (including each of the monotheistic traditions at various points in their histories), it is completely unknown in Neopagan circles. The only thing that comes even vaguely close are Wiccan legends about elderly Witches during World War II who supposedly died from exhaustion after putting too much of their mana into rituals intended to prevent Hitler from invading England. There is little, however, even vaguely resembling historical evidence that this event ever took place.

[††] Unless you're worshiping a hunting or war deity, when the hunters or warriors might shed a few symbolic drops of their *own* blood. Of course, even a drop of blood from a pinprick will offend some folks.

"LEND YOUR AID UNTO THE SPELL": CHANNELING ENERGY

Mana can be *tapped* or absorbed from natural or artificial environments, from the ether, from or via ceremonial tools and other charged objects, from the members of your congregation, and from cooperative spirits (when it sometimes becomes channeling, see below).

The term "tapping" is taken from the metaphor of tapping beer from a keg (a *tap* originally referred to the cork or spigot on such a keg). *Webster's* tells us that tapping means "to draw out, from, or upon," as in "tapping new sources of revenue." Tapping mana involves opening ourselves up to the presence of mana, making a psychic/magical/spiritual connection to it, then pulling the mana into us for theurgical or thaumaturgical purposes.‡‡

Physical nature is filled with mana, as anyone psychically sensitive notices almost immediately. It's most obvious in places such as the Grand Canyon, Carlsbad Caverns, Mount Kilimanjaro, Yosemite, or a redwood forest. In fact, it's the presence of such mana that makes many people want to treat these spots reverently, and which causes them to be turned into parks and preserves. When you are at Niagara Falls, Old Faithful geyser in Yellowstone National Park, Mont St. Michael's, an ocean beach, or outside during a thunderstorm or hurricane, the energy of the moving air and/or water seems to generate even more mana than that present at the quieter and less dramatic power spots. Places that have been used for many years as ceremonial sites often have strong mana stored within them, especially if artificial changes have been made to the land, such as the building of stone circles or pyramids. In general, the age of the site in its current form, the number of living plants and animals present, the amount of kinetic energy there, and the history of its use for magical/spiritual purposes, seem to be the major variables determining how much mana will be available.

---

‡‡ A usage I may have received from Randall Garrett, himself an expert on both magic and beer.

You won't need gigantic amounts of mana for most liturgies, which is why a cabin by a lake, a backyard with a couple of big trees, or a local park may be sufficient for your purposes. When you are indoors, however, don't miss the possibilities of tapping mana from a roaring hearth fire, an altar that has been used for a long time, or even from the electrical circuits in the walls.§§

The *ether* is defined by *The Encyclopedia Britannica* thusly: "a hypothetical substance filling all space, inclusive of those volumes occupied by ordinary matter, and serving to transmit those forces (gravitational, electric, magnetic) which one material object exerts on another located at a distance." The ether is an old-fashioned idea; belief in it changes from generation to generation of physicists. Currently it is sneaking its way back into respectable physics under a variety of names, most notably the "space-time continuum" and the "quantum field" (or perhaps now it's the "dark matter/dark energy" they're chasing).

The ether can be thought of as a very subtle or thin fog of some sort of unknown energy that ties all other known forms of energy (including psi) together—in which case it may be just another name for mana—or it can be thought of as the structure of space-time itself. Most traditional occult theories (at least in the West) declare the ether to be the lowest (closest to material reality) of what they call the "astral planes."

It's not necessary to believe in the ether to use the concept in your rituals. Merely assume that space itself (the ether) is full of mana, just as it is full of gravity near a planet, and that therefore you can pull mana out of thin air. However, while the ether *may* contain an infinite amount of mana, it is rarely concentrated, so tapping from it can take longer than tapping from other sources.

The amount of mana to be tapped *from* ceremonial tools is usually fairly small unless the object is very old and/or has been charged up with mana on multiple occasions. Instead, most sacred objects

---

§§ Be careful when tapping/transmuting the energy from wall circuits—if you aren't careful you can get a nasty shock.

are used as cuing devices to help a priest/ess, shaman, or medicine person to tap mana *through* them. This is especially true of icons, idols, and other artistic depictions of spirits, which are considered to have strong psychic/magical/spiritual connections to the spirits represented.

The clergy and the congregation generate most of the mana used in liturgies (at least until phase four). As we have seen, much of what happens in a liturgy (or any other group ritual) is specifically designed to raise mana of a particular flavor, so that the clergy can tap into that mana, focus or shape it, and use it for the congregation's needs.

Tapping the mana of spirits, whether nature spirits, elementals, ancestors, or deities, is part of what you are doing when you invoke (or sometimes evoke) a non-corporeal entity. Spirits, however, have consciousnesses of their own, which is why you can't simply plug into them as you can a waterfall, an electric circuit, or the ether. Indeed, Paleopagans would say that the line between spirits and inanimate objects is a fuzzy one, which is why you should be respectful—even when your mana source seems to be a nonconscious one.[¶¶]

As for channeling a deity, here's some of what I said in *Bonewits's Essential Guide to Witchcraft and Wicca* (Citadel, 2006):

> Once the circle is complete, there is often a ritual process of invocation or evocation known as "Drawing Down the Moon," which is usually done by the High Priest (HP)…upon the High Priestess (HPS)…The intent is that the High Priestess…will be able to manifest the Goddess to the coven through divine *inspiration, conversation, channeling,* or *possession.*

> In this context, *inspiration* refers to the reception of ideas from the Goddess which arrive as abstract concepts without any pseudo-sensory input, and which the HPS must then put into words of her own before passing them on. *Conversation* implies

---

¶¶ The knowledge of this fuzzy line leads to pantheism, panentheism, and animism, as discussed in Chapter 1.

that she *hears* the Goddess' voice (sometimes accompanied by a vision of her), can mentally converse with her, and specific phrases can then be passed on from the Goddess. *Channeling* (known a hundred years ago as "mediumship") means that the Goddess uses the High Priestess' vocal apparatus to speak directly with the others in what amounts to a light or *partial possession.*

In all of these levels of spirit communication, the High Priestess' awareness of her own spirit or soul is still in her physical body. In a total or *full possession,* however, she will usually leave her body while the Goddess controls it, and will often have no memory later of what her body was doing or saying while the deity was in it.

It should be clear that drawing down involves tapping mana from the deity, along with whatever wisdom she/he/it cares to share. Since the deities can be thought of as consisting of pure mana,*** they have a lot of power available. This can easily overwhelm an invoker (think about pouring fifty liters of water into a five-liter bucket), which is why one has to approach them carefully and learn how to handle the mana flows safely.††† When a deity or other spirit is perceived within the priest/ess, he/she can ask him/her/it for assistance with the rest of the liturgy or any magical workings or rites of passage to be performed—to "lend their aid unto the spell," in the words of an old Wiccan chant.

The above concept of channeling is distinct from a more casual one we might call *external channeling* of mana flows, in which the priest/ess or other magical worker shapes and focuses the mana as if it were water in an aqueduct or light going through a lens. This is usually easier on the consciousness than internal channeling would

---

*** See Chapter 2, The Nature of Deities and Vice Versa.

††† Perhaps the reason why most Neopagan drawings-down don't actually *work* is that the Deities understand how little prepared most modern Anglos are for channeling, let alone possession.

be. External channeling is what a priest/ess does when consecrating food and/or drink during the return phase of a liturgy. It involves learning to visualize (or otherwise sense/create) the flows of mana and the astral/imaginary containers, lenses, or other metaphors involved.

Which brings us to the following topic.

CONES OF POWER AND WORKING THROUGH THE CENTER

The idea of raising a *cone of power* (which may have its origins in the Spiritualist movement) is that the participants create, usually by dancing and/or chanting, a large, cone-shaped field of mana. When the energy builds to a peak, the cone is supposed to send the mana toward the target, carrying the power and information content of the spell. Nice theory. Unfortunately, most of the time it doesn't work.

Leave aside the rude comments I've previously made about Neopagan ceremonial dancing, and the fact that many Neopagans don't physically mark the edges of their ritual area, and thus have no clear idea of where the base of the cone is supposed to be. Ignore the fact that no two cone-raisers ever seem to agree about the size, shape (sharp or squat?), color, solidity or hollowness (if hollow, sides only or sides plus bottom?), etc. of their cone. These are all symptoms of the general lack of planning and training in a community composed primarily of newcomers. Instead, let's examine a different cluster of factors, those of physics and metaphysics.

In every generation, metaphors to describe magical, spiritual, and psychic events are taken from the latest major technology available. Neopagans, Spiritualists, and New Agers forty years ago tended, for example, to use metaphors taken from electromagnetic broadcasting technology, while current energy workers are more likely to use quantum metaphors. Let's look at spell casting or prayer with the earlier metaphor first, as mechanist as it might seem.

When you send a spell/prayer toward a distant target, whether in a focused straight line or vaguely in all directions, you are essentially either narrowcasting or broadcasting a message. Like any other message sent through normal space and time, it is subject to a deterioration of (a) its power level, (b) its directional vectors, and (c) its information content.

The further away your target is, the more power will be wasted simply in getting there. When it does arrive, it may not be strong enough to do much. If the target of a narrowcast moves, or you didn't really know where he/she/it was in the first place, or some other energy field deflects your beam, your spell or prayer may wind up missing the target completely. If the distance is great, the sheer psychic static of our biosphere (let alone deliberate efforts by others) can disrupt the psychic structure of your spell/ prayer, causing it to lose all or most of its information content. Even if it arrives on target with lots of power, it may well wind up doing little or nothing that you wanted done.

How do you get around the problem of a spell or prayer deteriorating when it goes via normal space and time? The answer is remarkably simple: you bypass normal space and time completely, by using the ritual center of your working area as a shortcut. You see, every ritual center is connected to every other ritual center, since in one sense they are all the same: each is the center of the cosmos.[74] If you have previously created a sacred space around the target of your spell, or if you create one symbolically at this point of the ceremony, you can establish (recognize, actually) a magical-psychic-spiritual connection between the ritual centers of both places.

A spell or prayer that you send into the center of your working area will arrive instantly at the center of the other location, without going through time or space as we know it. It will pop out of that other center with full power and information content, while the directional vectors will have become irrelevant. It won't matter if your target is ten miles or ten thousand miles away or even (note to my great-great-grandchildren) ten light years away.

One technique I have seen used successfully is to put a round, cut-glass crystal or matrix, in the center of your altar as a tool to focus the group's attention and into which they can pour their energies. If possible, try to have a similar crystal in the center of the location where the target of your spell/prayer happens to be. Putting it around a sick person's neck in a small bag will work just fine.

I first discovered the center-to-center technique by accident many years ago, when I was living in Berkeley, California and heard on the radio that the Canadian nesting grounds of an endangered species of birds were about to be engulfed by a forest fire. I had already noticed a 500-mile limit in my previous spell castings, and the distance involved was a couple of thousand miles, but I figured I had to do *something.* So I got out a map of Canada and drew a circle centered on the nesting grounds, then invoked Thor and did a rain spell. The circled map was in the middle of my altar, which was in the center of my working area. I cast the spell into the map and hoped for the best. Much to my surprise and delight, a few hours later I heard on the news that a rainstorm had come out of nowhere and stopped the forest fire a short distance away from the nesting grounds.

For years I thought it was the use of the map as a mandala (magical design) that had been the key, but eventually I figured out that the critical steps had been defining two ritual centers and then merging them. Of course, you might point out that the magical Law of Similarity, which prompted me to use a map in the first place, caused the map to *be* the endangered area, right there on my altar, and thus there was no distance to be traversed by my spell. I suspect that this center-to-center technique is in fact related to the Law of Similarity (and Contagion) and that each may shed light on the other.[75] I also suspect that this approach to spells/prayers is both ancient and well in keeping with quantum physics.

Obviously, with most rites of passage, or specific healings/blessings on people present in the circle, you are not going to be sending energies outside the boundaries of your current sacred space, but rather into the bodies/auras of folks right there. The precise wording of the ritual-within-the-ritual of a child blessing, ordination, coming of age, healing, etc., should provide everyone all the information they need to send or receive the energies.

Masculine vs. Feminine
Spell/Prayer Casting

Whether we are using a cone of power, the sacred center, or some other focusing metaphor, there appear to be two major approaches to generating and releasing mana, which can be correlated to a male/female polarity. The masculine approach seems to be one of building up energies higher and higher until they can't be contained anymore, then releasing them in a sudden burst of power, usually in a particular direction. The feminine approach seems to be one of generating and building continuous waves of energy, which are released, built up again, then released again, in a series of waves of energy sent in all directions.[‡‡‡]

Obviously, the former can be seen as conducive to narrowcasting and the latter to broadcasting of mana, while they can both be used with the center-to-center method and other focusing metaphors as well.

The ritual techniques in use by most modern Neopagans were created by people familiar with the rather macho styles of the renaissance ceremonial magicians and the members of the Hermetic Order of the Golden Dawn. Thus, even though women became the dominant leadership of the majority of Neopagan traditions, they still tend to use the approach I've labeled "masculine" here.

The masculine approach seems, in my experience, to work best for ritual goals that can be accomplished with a sudden burst of mana arriving swiftly to change the targets' energy patterns, while the feminine approach seems to work best with goals that need for their targets to receive multiple gentle floods of mana to produce the desired results. A mixed approach, of course, would work best for situations that require an initial burst, followed by waves, as in certain cancer healings.

Now come the necessary disclaimers when waltzing into the gender minefield: I am *not* saying that either end of the feminine-to-masculine polarity spectrum is superior to the other in any absolute

---

[‡‡‡]   Does this remind you of anything?

way when it comes to energy control in ritual. *Nor* am I saying that all or most men do or should do the building and release of mana a certain way, while all or most women do or should do it in the other manner. What I *am* saying is that your participants' tendencies to prefer either approach to building and releasing mana in ritual should guide you in designing a liturgy and a spell/prayer-casting method that will satisfy the greatest number of parties, as well as be most effective in fulfilling their goals.

When Not to Raise Power or Do Magic

When you do spell castings or rites of passage at the return stage of the liturgy,§§§ you should have no need to generate more power, since everyone should already have as much deity-given power in them as they can handle. Instead, use chants, talismans, and gestures[76] as devices to focus your visualization, timing, and power. That way, everyone can release their divinely enhanced power at the same instant, toward a uniformly visualized target, with a unified intent, to achieve the agreed-upon goal.

Beyond the question of when to raise mana, is that of when to do *or avoid doing* magic. Most books on magic won't tell you this, but often magic is *not* the best answer to a problem. Before you do a theurgical or thaumaturgical working, you should make sure that magic is really necessary. Most problems can be solved with less drama, but more effect, by mundane means. Magic is there to give you an edge, to improve the odds in your favor—not to substitute for all other human activity.

I suggest not doing magic or bothering deities with requests until after you've tried *all* other ethical means to solve your problem. At that point, your awareness that magic is your last option will add a great deal of emotional power, and thus mana, to your efforts when you decide to take spiritual action.

---

§§§   See Chapter 3, Phase Four.

Even if magic is necessary in a situation, it is seldom sufficient. Fertility spells won't help the crops much if you neglect to weed and water the fields. A prosperity spell is unlikely to do much if you're too lazy to work. A spell to heal the Earth is useless if you can't be bothered to fight the polluters and destroyers by physical, economic, and/or political means as well. Too many people use religious and magical rituals as an excuse to avoid hard, Earth-plane level *work*.

10

A Modular Approach to Liturgical Design

A Cybernetic Metaphor

Aidan Kelly once pointed out that:

> ...In a properly constructed ritual, there is no deadwood, no filler; rather, every word, every line, every action, every object used, contributes its weight towards achieving the purpose of the ritual. Obviously, in order to achieve such elegance and efficiency, you must thoroughly understand every detail of the ritual, and in order to achieve such understanding, you must construct the ritual in detail, from the ground up.[77]

It's now time to discuss the exact procedure for creating ceremonies. What I call *modular liturgical design* is an approach inspired by computer programming techniques. Before anyone complains that computers are neither magical nor religious, let me point out that a computer program *can* be seen as a type of ritual. A program is an ordered sequence of events (in this case, instructions to be executed), meant to be followed the same way each time. It is designed to produce a predictable (altered?) state of consciousness inside the computer (decision making), within which certain desired results (decisions) can be obtained. Perhaps it's a strained metaphor, but following it has led to some interesting breakthroughs in liturgical design.

In the early days of computer programming it was common to begin at the beginning and continue until you reached the end. Thousands of lines of instructional computer codes would be written, the program would be run, and it would crash (fail completely). A guess would be made as to the reasons for the crash, parts of the code would be rewritten, the program would be run again, and it would crash. This would go on for a very long time until eventually a working program would be put together with the logical equivalents of chewing gum and baling wire.

This is similar to how most Neopagan liturgists work. Generally, they start at the beginning of a ritual script, write it straight through, and then try it (usually without rehearsal). Each subsequent script by the same liturgist will contain modifications designed to correct the perceived mistakes (if any were actually noticed) from the last time. Since the rewrites are usually done once a month or once every six weeks, it can take years before a liturgy has been completely debugged (if it ever is), and long before then, it's become a fossilized tradition, and people aren't allowed to make any more changes.

Eventually people in the computer industry began to realize that breaking a large program down into byte-sized pieces would make it more manageable and testable. By taking an over-all or *top-down* look at a proposed program first, then dividing it up into sections, subsections, and sub-subsections, even the most intimidating of projects could be organized into a coherent set of steps. The smallest logical clumps of programming (such as codes for the CPU* to receive input from a keyboard, or to look for a printer, for example) were called *modules*. A programmer would write the code for a module, test it to see if it worked, then combine it with another module that had been previously tested. If the *linkage* (the connecting computer codes) between the two bits of programming was good, then another module could be written, tested, connected, and its linkage tested. Eventually

---

* "Central Processing Unit," the main "chip" that controls the computer.

several modules would be combined into a single subsection of the over-all program, subsections into sections, and all the sections into one coherent whole.

The primary advantage of this top-down or modular programming technique is that when a program crashes or needs to be modified, it's comparatively easy to zero in on the offending module, make a few small changes, and have it all work properly. Further, modules that work well in one program can be recycled to do the same job in another one, without having to start from scratch each time. All of this has revolutionized computer programming and made possible most of the programs we have today.

The modular approach to liturgical design works in a very similar fashion. You start by doing a complete pattern analysis on your proposed ceremony, breaking it down into a handful of major sections of ritual activity, and each of these into subsections and sub-subsections. You might even consider drawing a flow chart showing the path from each stage of the rite to the next, as well as decision points to switch to contingency plans.[†]

Then pick a few related sub-subsections and create them. Test each individually to see how it looks/sounds/feels. Fiddle with them until each module works just the way you want, then create something that links two of them together. The linkage can be temporal (picking an order to do the modules in) and/or spatial (designating exactly where, physically, the modules will be done, in relation to each other) and/or conceptual (creating words, music, or other sounds and sights that will tie the basic idea of each module together with that of the others). Test to see how well these two modules work together, then change your linkage as necessary. Attach more modules together, testing the linkage in each case, then try performing all the modules in this subsection of your liturgy, and observe the results.

When you're satisfied with the first subsection, proceed to create and test other subsections in the same way. Eventually, you can link the subsections into sections, test linkages individually and collectively,

---

† See below.

then merge the sections into the liturgy as a whole. This then is tested in the rehearsals before the first full performance.

When doing the testing, make sure to pay attention to the pacing of each part, and remember the effects that different-sized congregations will have on various activities (if passing food or drink among twenty people takes five minutes, doing it with two hundred people can take half an hour).

Just as with modular programming, this technique of liturgical design takes longer to create the first full version of a ceremony. But it has the same advantage that modular programming has, of making it easier to change and expand the results. And just as programmers build up a library of programming modules that they can use over and over again, so too can a liturgical designer build up a library of ritual modules that can be combined in a variety of ways in later ceremonies.

Examples of Modular Liturgical Design

Suppose you are creating a Celtic-style liturgy in which you need at some point early on to open the Gates Between the Worlds. You create a procedure for one or two of your ritual participants to do this, say by singing a chant in Gaelic, making a particular gesture with a particular magical tool, and visualizing a Celtic spiral opening. You test different versions of the song, different gestures with different tools, and different versions of the spiral. Eventually you settle on the combination you like, figure out the exact order and spatial locations you want, wrap some Celtic music around it (to provide part of the conceptual linking), and try it *without* full psychic power.[‡] Then you can proceed to create and test the other parts of your liturgy that happen before and after the gate opening, then the entire first quarter or third of your liturgy (including the gate opening), then the entire ritual.

The next time you are creating a liturgy that requires a gate opening part, but it happens to be a Norse rite, you can start out with

---

‡ In this particular example, you don't want to test it with full power until after you've created and tested a full-powered gate *closing!*

the basic pattern you already have for the Celtic opening. You might translate the song to Icelandic (or write a new song entirely), keep the gesture but do it with a more Norse type of magical tool, visualize a Norse sort of gate image instead of the spiral, use Swedish music to tie it all together, etc. The result will be that you can re/create your Norse gate opening in a fraction of the time it took to write the first one, since you are working with well-tested and familiar modules. Provided that the cultural and aesthetic themes don't clash within or between the modules of your design, you can borrow bits and pieces from a dozen previous ceremonies created according to this approach, and put them into a new liturgy with amazing speed. Eventually you'll acquire a liturgical design library of ritual modules (processionals, gate openings, invocations, consecrations, etc.) that can be carefully mixed and matched (via the linking procedures) to meet whatever future design needs may pop up.

Many Neopagan liturgists do part of this process already, in that they will borrow and reuse favorite prayers, chants, etc. Unfortunately, they do it without the pattern analysis, linking and testing procedures just mentioned. Most of the time some ritual design created years ago is repeated (because it's traditional) and the favorite items are inserted willy-nilly. The results are usually chaotic and confusing, without a smooth energy flow from start to finish, without a group mind being created and reinforced, and without the psychic/spiritual forces actually going where they are supposed to. These cannot be considered successful ceremonies, no matter how much fun people had putting them on.

The Advantages of Repeating Patterns/Motifs

Just as in writing a symphony or opera, repeated patterns or *motifs* can tie an entire work together artistically, and thus magically. The cultural and aesthetic themes of your liturgy, for example, can provide multiple ideas for making the ceremony appear unified. Particular verbal or musical phrases, deity names, or images can be used repeatedly to great effect.

For example, in liturgies done by some modern Druids, a series of preliminary invocations of other spirits will be done before the main invocation of the deity(ies) of the occasion.[78] The bardic spirit, nature spirits, ancestors, and other deities are each collectively asked to "join us in the worship of Danu and the Dagda" (or whoever). This repetition layers the ideas one upon the other and leads to increased anticipation of the main invocation.

Another example would be the repeated use of the four classical elements in a Wiccan liturgy, with repeated words for blessing the elemental tools, doing the invocations to the four directions, etc. Additionally, in quarter invocations you can use lines that are largely similar for each direction, but which vary in a predictable, elementally appropriate, manner (as discussed in Chapter 8).

The Importance of Contingency Planning

This isn't a matter of knowing what to do when things go wrong,[§] so much as it is one of making plans to handle probable variations in your liturgical situation. For example, if you don't know how many people will be arriving for your ceremony, plan how the script will change according to the population: "If we have less than 20, we'll pass the main cup around during the return; for 20–40, we'll pass two extra cups; for 40–100, we'll pass four cups and do a longer chant; for over 100, or if there's a flu virus going around, we'll forget about cups and asperge everyone instead."

Go through the outline of your liturgy and look to see how changing situations could alter your plans. Have an indoor version of your outdoor ritual ready in case of a major rainstorm, with waterproof direction signs to tell latecomers where to go. Have a way to do your ritual without an open fire if the park rangers say there's a serious forest fire hazard. If the folks who are supposed to run the ceremony haven't shown up with the props, an hour after the ritual was to have started, gather together everyone present who has some experience and see who has what materials

---

§   See that discussion in Chapter 12.

with them, then start without the experts—the ritual must go on! The "stars" will show up on time in the future.

Well, okay, sometimes it won't be appropriate to continue with a ceremony. By and large, however, if it is at all possible and appropriate to do so, perform whatever rite has been planned and scheduled.

ORTHODOXY VS. CREATIVITY

There are advantages and disadvantages to doing liturgies within a tradition—whether it be two, twenty, or two hundred years old. Having your liturgies fit within a familiar orthodox pattern will certainly add to the important sensation of continuity that is affirmed in most rites. While orthodoxy means "correct practice," being politically or liturgically correct, if done in a heavy-handed way, can stifle creativity or even common sense. The wise liturgist will discover ways to be creative within the constraints of her or his religious traditions.

As Driver puts it:

> The liminality [or spiritually transitional quality] of rituals means that they are informed, on the one hand, by a greater than usual sense of order and, on the other, by a heightened sense of freedom and possibility. Being imaginative, rituals can experiment with both ideal order and ideal freedom, releasing feelings of love and participation in the process. Being playful, rituals can afford to fail. Freedom from the tyranny of having to succeed enhances, paradoxically, the likelihood of their achieving their goal.[79]

Of course, the freedom to fail is strongest with rituals that are primarily theurgical rather than thaumaturgical. If a liturgy is done to honor the Rain deities and thereby produce rain, it can't really be considered an unimportant failure if the drought continues!

Just as it is possible to write beautiful poems within the centuries-old structure of a sonnet, so too can beautiful liturgies be created and performed within the tight structural bounds of an ancient liturgical tradition.

Liturgies that include rites of passage, such as initiations or weddings, should have as much traditional material in them as possible, tempered by the needs of those who are the primary focus. Rites of intensification, such as holiday celebrations, on the other hand, may profitably be modified to fit the circumstances (weather, local news, etc.) of the actual day or night they are performed.

Rigid liturgical structures are often used to maintain orthodoxy on other issues, especially if preservation of a religious establishment is more important than the individual spiritual welfare of the members. Contrarily, ceremonies that are always made up as they go along may be done that way to hide the ignorance or incompetence of the ritual's leaders.

Phaedra has some pithy words on the topic of coerced creativity. Speaking to a group of feminist spirituality practitioners, she said:

> Find a middle ground. Some women's circles have created a tyranny of creativity. Every ritual has to be original and more creative than the one before. The members wind up exhausted! Novelty for the sake of novelty accomplishes nothing. If you find something that works, stick with it. It's okay to repeat things you've done before; it's okay to repeat whole rituals.[80]

For example, my Pagan Way study group started a particular custom for Yule rituals several years ago, passing flames from candle to candle in a certain way and singing a particular song. Now, if we do a Yule ceremony without doing those two things, it just doesn't feel like Yule to us! These are the sorts of traditions that, however randomly begun, end up creating a strong group identity that can last for years.

Contrarily, "If it ain't broke, don't fix it!" In other words, don't casually remove or change a part of a successful ceremony if you don't know why it was there to begin with. Track down the people who originally created the ceremony (which is easier if they are both alive and non-mythical) and *ask them* why they did what they did. Then you can change it after you have figured out how you are going to get the same effect or have decided you don't need that effect after all.

11

PREPARING FOR A RITUAL

There are many different aspects to preparing for a liturgy, including intellectual, artistic, practical, physical, emotional, social, and psychic activities and issues. In this chapter we'll look at the most important of these, in a roughly chronological order.

PLANNING SESSIONS

Even if you are using a traditional script with no modifications (something I don't recommend), you still need to make additional plans. Get the folks who intend to take part together at least two weeks beforehand. Assign roles, responsibilities for preparation work, duties to bring specific supplies, etc. Decide on a theme for the rite, and thus on the colors, symbols, deities, and songs to use. Decide if more research into the deities and/or the occasion might be needed, and who will do it. Choose the exact place and time for the rehearsals and the ritual itself, if and how its going to be publicized, and how everyone and everything will be transported to the rehearsals and the ceremony.

Making all these decisions may take more than one session. If your group has regular weekly or biweekly meetings, you can incorporate this planning into them, spending more time on it as you get closer to the actual date. Otherwise, you should schedule at least two planning sessions, one for making the decisions just listed, and the other to hand out scripts, song lyrics, driving maps, etc. Try to give everyone enough time to memorize their parts, since ceremonies always look better without scripts and cue cards being visible.

Casting

Cast the most qualified folks available for each role. The idea is not to be snobbish, but to exercise at least as much discretion in casting as your local little theater group or community chorus. Don't give the role of chief bard to someone who can't play his/her instrument adequately, or sing on the pitch, when someone competent is available. If parts of a ceremony are in another language and there's only one person around who can correctly pronounce the Irish (or Welsh, or Polish, or Norse, etc.), let her or him do the words in that language. If that person is not an experienced or competent ritualist, pair them up with someone who is. If you're going to do a ritual drama or dance in the middle of the rite, get people who know how to do it well.

If you have a small group with only five or six people working in it, then you can't be so picky. Assume that you're all growing in your arts and pass the available roles around as democratically as you like, but as soon as your group begins to have twenty or thirty people, you're going to want to start selecting and training specific individuals to take on more responsibility. Newcomers who want to perform major roles in the rituals should be tested and (if competent) immediately drafted.

Beware of nepotism! Your spouse, lover, or best friend may not be the right person for a particular role, no matter how much you love them. The owner of the ritual site is not automatically qualified to be the presiding clergyperson. A member who makes a large donation to your group's expenses should not be casually handed an important role that he or she is not competent to fill. Special thanks, blessings, or social positions may be given to people of these sorts, but personal preferences (or animosities) should not be allowed to interfere with giving the deities, and the members of your group, the best possible ceremonies.

Cupbearers/aspergers are necessary for medium- or larger-sized groups. Ritual dance and theater sequences require dancers and actors. If you have banners, you may want people to be banner holders. If you expect that unfriendly outsiders may disturb your ritual, you may also want to have a few warrior types with quarterstaffs guarding the perimeters of your site.* You may also want them to take responsibility for helping anyone who has a medical or psychological problem during the ceremony (in which case they should know what they're doing).

Any ceremony with a medium-sized or larger group needs to have some people, let's call them chant facilitators, who really do know all the chants and songs well, and who can deliver them loudly enough to lead the rest of the congregation. Perhaps your group's chief bard may select and train these people, and you may want them to have some distinctive symbol or article of clothing (then the pre-ritual briefing can include something like "listen to the people with the blue sashes, they know all the songs.") You should have one chant facilitator for every ten people, but they can also be taking other duties, such as being cupbearers, provided that they remain evenly distributed around the area whether moving or standing, and keep singing or chanting throughout.

Each of the major roles should have understudies (who can double as chant facilitators). Not only is this a good way for less-experienced members of your group to learn your customs, but can be a Goddess-send when one of your major officers is suddenly called out of town or gets the plague. And if one of the understudies winds up doing a better job of memorizing and performing the ceremony than the person originally cast, then she or he should be given the part. Yes, there will be screaming about this. But if your group is really interested in

---

* These should be people with extremely cool heads, unless you have lots of money to spare for lawsuits.

ceremonial excellence, then they are going to have to be able to sub-ordinate their artistic egos to the cause of better ceremonies.

Above all, when selecting people to handle functions in a large public ritual, remember yet again: "Sincerity is not a substitute for competence."

Diet and Drugs

Good nutrition is very important in maintaining your alertness and stamina. If your ceremony is to be short, you'll want to avoid having red meat or other heavy foods in your stomach when you start. If it's going to be a long ritual, you may want to eat a good solid meal a couple of hours beforehand.

There are a number of authorities, both western and eastern, who highly recommend that all magic users should maintain a vegetarian diet. Perhaps because humans evolved as omnivores, removing all red meat from your diet does tend to loosen your connection to the Earth plane and to make you more sensitive to the flows of mana within yourself and the others around you.

As for drugs, a small dose of caffeine, sugar, and/or chocolate may be useful to some people just before the ritual begins. Others find that alcohol in very small amounts is useful for reducing pre-ceremonial jitters. However, large amounts of any of these drugs can ruin your timing, and excess alcohol can affect your memory and make you miss cues. As with everything else in magic and religion, common sense, moderation, and paying attention to the unique character-istics of each person involved will usually be your best guides.

Alcohol, as mentioned before, is the primary ritual drug used in western mainstream religions, and is therefore not thought of as a drug in those circumstances. Tobacco is popular for religious use among Native Americans, as are several other plants such as sage, datura, and various funny mushrooms. Middle Eastern and Asian re-ligions have used cannabis and opium products in worship ceremo-nies for millennia.

It has been my experience that psychedelic drugs are useless for most ceremonies other than vision quests, which are not liturgies. Of course, if your ritual is one of a small group worshipping a "plant deva" such as San Mescalito (peyote), the White Lady (belladonna), the Mushroom Lord (amanita muscaria), etc., then it will be appropriate to use the organic drug that the spirit rules, but these drugs are extremely dangerous and often illegal. They should only be used under the supervision of an experienced, trained psychopomp, in a legal jurisdiction where their consumption will not get anyone arrested, and never by minors.† The worship of the deity should not be merely an excuse to indulge in the drug; rather the drug should be a sacrament that enables the deity's worshippers to attain a closer communion with him/her.

Many people feel that they need drugs to enable them to loosen up enough to see and manipulate mana properly. Most of these people are fooling themselves and/or have not had competent teachers. I've seen drug use mess up far more ceremonies than I have ever seen it enhance.

The bottom line on both drugs and diet is that what some people may find to be a useful tool, others may find a dangerous trap.

Site Preparation

The overwhelming majority of Neopagans and other members of minority belief systems do not own their own real estate (one of the reasons that mainstream churches often look down on us). If you are lucky enough to have land with a temple or sacred grove already established, much of this section can be skipped. However, for those of you who will be using land you do not control, or renting a hall, several steps (some of which have been previously mentioned) need to be taken long before the ritual is begun.

Scout out the location in which you intend to perform your ceremony several days before the ritual is scheduled. See where the light

---

† Swooping SWAT teams can really ruin the ambiance of a sacred ceremony.

and/or shade is likely to fall at the scheduled time, as well as the views in different directions (what tree is the sun going to rise over?). Check out the acoustics to see if that bagpipe is really practical. See if there are game players or amorous teenagers who customarily use the same spot at the scheduled time. Find out if civil authorities (city police, park rangers, etc.) need to be notified ahead of time, or permits obtained. If possible, do most of this before the first rehearsal.

If you are going to have an outdoor fire, see to it that someone who knows what she or he is doing has been appointed as fire warden. Let her/him apply for any required permits (often separate from land use permits), set up a proper fire pit, and arrange for the necessary firefighting tools to be available.

The day of the event will bring you its own tasks, depending upon whether the ritual is to be done outdoors or indoors. Outdoors, clear the ground of sharp rocks, twigs, etc. If a permanent altar is in place, clear the leaves and animal droppings from it. Garden torches or hurricane lamps can be set in place around the perimeter as needed.

When working indoors, make sure before the ritual begins that the telephone is unplugged and "Do not disturb" signs are on the outside doors. Tell everyone to set their cell phones, pagers, or other electronic devices to silent running. Turn off any noisy air conditioners, heating systems, or smoke alarms that are otherwise likely to roar into action during the rite. Be sure to reconnect everything afterward.

Outdoors or in, your working area should be clearly marked. No matter what else you will be doing, you will be creating an area in which mana fields will be generated and directed. The boundaries within which this activity will take place will normally need to be obvious to the conscious and subconscious minds of the participants. In my experience, there is no substitute for your working area being surrounded by a clearly visible line (or group of lines) marking the edges of a circle, triangle, square, etc.[81]

Outdoors, this can be accomplished by dropping powdered chalk, flour, or cornmeal (the last two being very biodegradable) onto the ground, cutting thin strips of turf (to be replaced after the ritual), drawing in the sand of a beach with staves, etc. Indoors, you can put tape or paint on a floor, lay out ribbon, cord, or even wooden strips on carpeting, etc. The point is to make it really obvious on the Earth plane level of reality when a person is or is not in the sacred space.

Ritual Tools

Most people trained in the western mainstream occult tradition and its offshoots think of chalices and swords, wands and censers, and similar such items in this category, although many other sorts of items can be (and have been) used for ritual purposes. It's important to make sure that all the necessary major tools for your rite are clean, present, and in working order (blades sharp, metal polished, etc.). Yet minor tools and trivial aspects of the major ones can become sources of extreme inconvenience if they haven't been properly prepared and laid out.

The placement of tools should be tested during rehearsals. You don't want folks tripping over drums, or knocking flower vases over, or not being able to see the wand because it's slipped under the sword, etc. Are you going to be using a staff? Where will you put it during the times you aren't gesturing with it—or will you be making all your gestures one-handed? Is something hot on the altar likely to set something else on fire? Will the bell be constantly banging against the cauldron when you lift or replace either one? Is your flute likely to roll off the not-quite-level altar-top? Working out all of these details ahead of time can save you a world of embarrassment later.

Food and Drink Utensils

Almost all Neopagan ceremonies, and most mainstream ones, include the sharing of food and/or drink. This is an area where both population and health factors need to be taken into account. With a small group, all of whom are known to be in good health (i.e., with no contagious conditions), the main chalice or drinking horn can be passed around. If the main cup has alcoholic liquid in it and you have teetotalers in your group, a secondary cup of spring water should also be passed (not juice, unless you know for certain that no tee-totaler present is allergic to its contents). You can generally assume that this will be necessary with a medium- or larger-sized group, or a small group where not everyone knows each other. If the presiding clergy have colds (or other unpopular viruses), both of the main cups should stay at the altar and additional ones be passed (consecration energies should be directed into all the vessels in these cases). Each participant can then drink from either or both containers, and pass them on.

With a medium-sized or larger group, it's safest to assume that at least some of them have a cold, flu or other virus that should not be shared along with the consecrated liquids. The main cup(s) should usually stay on the altar and larger vessels (such as cauldrons, pitchers, etc.), should be filled and consecrated along with the main cup(s). Under these circumstances, you'll want to tell people in your early announcements (and perhaps your processional songs at a festival) that they should each bring their own ritual cup. These can then be filled from the larger vessels of alcoholic and nonalcoholic fluids carried around by cupbearers.

Another reason to consecrate bigger vessels, such as cauldrons, is so they can be used to asperge large groups. With a small- or medium-sized group, passing cups around is not a major problem, but with large groups, the amount of time required for each participant to meaningfully partake can slowly add up, to the point where it destroys the ritual's pacing. For this reason, small cauldrons filled with spring water can be consecrated along with the main cup, then taken around the circle by assistants, who asperge the congregation with a bundle of twigs from a ritually appropriate tree or bush. This is not quite as effective as drinking the consecrated liquids would be, but with more than forty people, it may be necessary. However, if you have many cupbearers available, you could try having each one fill up the cups of a small segment of the congregation (such as an eighth of the circle) instead of asperging.

An important aesthetic note here is that all the cups, plates, and other drinking and eating utensils should be of good quality. I'm not talking about gold chalices studded with diamonds and rubies,[‡] but rather that these magical/religious tools should be impressive to the artistic and symbolic sensibilities of the users. If you are uncertain about how many people will be attending, you may be forced to have paper cups and plates on hand, but for Goddess' sake, have them at least look dignified.[§]

If possible, all of these drinking vessels or plates (large or small) should be of horn, stoneware, metal, wood, or other natural substances, and be used only for ritual purposes. They do not have to match, however the one(s) for nonalcoholic liquids should be very distinctive in appearance. If all you have is a set of identical vessels (or if none of them match each other), try putting silver or blue ribbons around the one(s) containing nonalcoholic liquids and gold or red ribbons around the alcoholic one(s). Generally, the proportion of alcoholic to nonalcoholic vessels should be one-to-one. If in doubt, it's better to err on the side of caution and have extra vessels and cupbearers.

As for passing food around during a ritual, many of the same problems hold. Eating takes time, and with a large group can demolish your carefully crafted pacing. You need to think about the physical (as well as the psychic) effects of the food you are using. If you are passing very dry crackers or cookies around, you'll want to make sure that the food goes to each person before the liquid does, so they can wash down their consecrated cookies with some magical milk.

Decide on the purpose of your sacred meal (strengthening or grounding, communion or celebration?) before you write it into your script, then make sure that the practical aspects don't wind up outweighing the spiritual ones. Certainly the very process of passing out and consuming food usually grounds the participants rather than charging them up, and the same holds for passing out drink to individual cups, unless it is done very swiftly.

---

‡ As if anyone other than a giant multinational corporation with a history of centuries of greed could afford such things.

§ Using styrofoam is probably a sin.

Rehearsals

Oh yes! As should be clear from all the earlier references, you need to have at least one full-dress rehearsal for any new or complex ritual, especially if you want to avoid some of the problems already mentioned. For a lengthy ceremony, you may want to have two or three rehearsals, with possible additional work for the singers, musicians, dancers, etc. I've heard complaints about rehearsals for years, but there is no escaping it—almost all of the really powerful, beautiful, and effective large group rituals I have ever participated in had plenty of rehearsal.¶ Folks who are unable or unwilling to rehearse have chosen their priorities, and have thus decided to be part of the congregation rather than clergy or bards.

Your final dress rehearsal is the time for any desired photos and recordings to be made. That way you can ban photographers and audio/videotapers from the ritual itself (unless they have long distance lenses and mikes). No ceremony and no person (whether clergy or congregation) should ever be filmed without the express permission of all parties concerned, no matter how popular or famous the cameraperson happens to be. The use of ceremonial masks by shy participants is an option for large rituals when the majority has agreed to be recorded/filmed.

Why so much fuss over this? Because (a) cameras (especially with flashes) and microphones are intrusive and disruptive both aesthetically and emotionally, and (b) homicidal organizations and individuals are perfectly capable of getting copies of photos and recordings and then using these to identify members of minority religions they wish to persecute. It's happened in the past and will again in the future. As a clergyperson, it's your responsibility to make sure that the egotistic, journalistic, or archival needs of some do not outweigh the ceremonial or survival needs of your congregation.

¶ Those that didn't had something else—like a solar eclipse—that was able to overwhelm all the other factors. Can *you* arrange eclipses?

When rehearsing rituals, do *not* do them with full emotional, and therefore full spiritual/magical/psychic, power. This can be tricky. Key invocations, chants, and trance inductions should be rehearsed in isolation when establishing that the words are correctly memorized, then have (neutral, not funny) nonsense words inserted during full rehearsals.

Ceremonial Baths

It's usually a good idea to do some sort of personal cleansing before starting any kind of ceremony. Why? As mentioned before,** there's nothing spiritually unclean about the average Neopagan. Yet, on the practical, Earth plane level of reality, if your hands are full of axle grease, you're going to leave permanent fingermarks on your robe. If you've been engaging in some strenuous activity that has left you covered with sweat, the odors wafting from your body are likely to compete with the incense. If you're feeling dirty, oily, or gritty, you're going to have a much harder time concentrating on relaxing and opening yourself up to the spiritual energies to be invoked.

Thus, I always recommend that people (especially clergy) take a shower or (preferably) a long, hot, soaking bath before doing a ceremony.

A common practice is to bless a handful of salt and mix it into the water, thus exorcising the water of any energies other than cleansing ones. You might want to mix crushed herbs or tiny amounts of aromatherapy oils into the bath and breathe in their odors while you bathe. Play soothing music on a machine, burn appropriate incense, light a candle, or add any other elements you like that will reinforce two primary ideas: (1) getting rid of all previous thoughts and concerns, and (2) beginning to focus on the energies to be worked with in the upcoming rite.

When you get out of the water, put on clean clothing, whether it's traveling clothes or your actual ceremonial garb (which should have

---

** In Chapter 3, Phase One.

been cleaned and/or ironed beforehand).†† Then go straight to the ritual site without letting your mind drift too far into other topics.

Individual Emotional States

A ceremony will work best if the participants begin in an emotional state similar to that which the ritual is supposed to reflect. Getting into the appropriate mood should be part of the pre-ritual meditations (see below) of all participants, but is especially important for the presiding clergy and bards. Members of the congregation can go with the flow during a rite, but the clergy and bards must keep a portion of their consciousness separate, even during the most emotionally intense moments, so that they can keep track of and guide the energy flow of the ritual as a whole. If this necessary separation is not to be emotionally and spiritual distressing to them, they must saturate the rest of their consciousness thoroughly with the mood(s) that they intend to create within the congregation.

Anyone who is in a particularly foul mood, whether of anger, fear, depression, pain, etc., should not participate in a magical or religious ceremony without warning at least some of the other participants, including the presiding clergy. Otherwise, they are likely to poison the group mind's emotional focus and/or disrupt its psychic unity. This does not mean that people in need should be abandoned or banished from the community's rituals. On the contrary, it means that a special effort should be made (either before the ceremony, or very early on in it) to cheer them up or, if appropriate, to encourage them to share their emotions with the congregation in a way that gives the unhappy person meaningful psychological support and which restores their sense of belonging to the group. They can then participate in at least a neutral, if not positive way.

---

†† In some faiths, there are specific prayers and meditations to be done while dressing in your ritual vestments.

SOCIAL FACTORS

The more activities of any sort that a group engages in together, the more effective their liturgical interactions will be.‡‡ Friends who see each other frequently are going to create a more unified group mind than an equal number of people who barely know each other. It used to be that people made their religious group the center of their social lives, and thus their abilities to create a group mind were more powerful and effective. This is one of the reasons why people who live in large cities, with many social distractions available, often have more difficulty creating and maintaining working ritual groups.

In any social group, tight or loose, you're going to have problems arise between the members. Intra-group and inter-group politics, personality clashes, and tumultuous love relationships can wreak havoc with your efforts to create a group mind for a ceremony. This is where the clergyperson needs all of her or his psychological and social skills to prevent such problems from destroying a ritual before it starts. If two or more members of the group are having a conflict, or someone shows up who is actively disliked by most of the membership, or the ceremony is an open, ecumenical one with people from feuding groups likely to show up, the presiding clergy need to deal with the situation quickly and effectively, yet compassionately. It may be necessary to tell warring parties that they are all banned from your rite. This can be one of the hardest tasks that a clergyperson ever faces, yet evading it will ruin even the most beautifully designed and executed liturgy.

For that matter, if you arrive at a liturgy and find someone there you can't stand, you should probably turn around and go home, because your hostility or distress may ruin the ritual for everyone else by impeding the creation and maintenance of the group mind. And no, that's not fun or fair.

---

‡‡ See Chapter 4, Intra-Group Familiarity.

Pre-Ritual Meditations

The presiding clergy and the bard(s) who will be most responsible for directing the energy flow of the ritual should spend at least fifteen minutes to half an hour in meditation before the ritual starts. Such meditation would consist of getting into the appropriate mood, grounding and centering, dwelling upon the theme of the rite, contemplating their ceremonial tools, reviewing their relationships with the deities of the occasion, etc. The purpose of all of this is to clear their minds of every nonritual thought, so that they can concentrate on the work they are about to do. The ceremonial bath is a good time and place for such preparatory meditations. If you're going to have a long processional, that can serve a similar purpose in starting the group focus. But you should not go from a casual social or party atmosphere directly into a ceremonial one, unless the ritual is of a specifically celebratory nature, such as a Yule festival or a wedding.

So others should take care of trivial and routine matters while the senior clergy are meditating. If there are no trained subordinates in the group, or if you have a very small group, the presiding clergy can announce a five-minute meditation break, five minutes before they intend to start. Encourage everyone to be silent and to make themselves ready for the ceremony. While they're doing that, the clergy can get some meditation of their own accomplished, perhaps while putting the final touches on the altar. In fact, even with a larger congregation, such an announcement and preparation period isn't a bad idea.

Pre-Ritual Briefings and Warmups

When everyone has gathered at the site, someone other than the presiding clergy should tell them (1) any parts of the ceremony that have been changed at the last minute, (2) any chants, song choruses, or litany responses with which they may not be familiar, (3) who will be responsible for what duties during the ceremony, (4) which cup(s) will hold non-alcoholic liquid, (5) any controversial symbolism or mythology to be used, etc.—in short, all the facts they need to know to participate fully. Some clergy like to tell people to stretch their muscles and warm up their voices during the briefing. This can lead to greater relaxation and better singing, both of which are valuable. But don't make your pre-ritual briefing so long that people wind up experiencing the ceremony twice! That's why it's called a *briefing*.

Sometimes a processional may occur before all the members of the congregation have arrived on the ritual site. This could happen, for example, at a festival, with participants joining the processional as it winds along its path, rather than everyone starting out at a set location. In that case, the pre-ritual announcements will need to be made after the processional has arrived and the people have distributed themselves into their intended places. This style of briefing should be fairly formal and dignified, so as to not disrupt whatever spiritual energies have already been raised among the congregation.

12

Some Tips for Effective Ritual Performance

Giving the Gods a Good Show

Even the best modern ceremonies, whether mainstream or minority—
the ones that people may talk about for weeks and months afterward—fall far short of what they *could* be. As we have seen, excessive
courtesy, interpersonal and intergroup politics, lack of fundamental
psychic and magical training, and childhood conditioning that one
doesn't criticize religious ceremonies, all conspire to make people
reluctant to voice their doubts about the rituals in common use in
their communities. Without those doubts being expressed, no improvements are likely to be made. Furthermore, simple ignorance of
what *strong* mana feels like has meant that many people never know
what it is they're missing.

Throughout this book, I've referred to the *performance* of a ritual and
made numerous other references to the theatrical and musical aspects
of ceremonies. A lifetime of experience has shown me that the artistic elements of a ritual, and most especially the musical and dramatic
ones, can be *the* critical determinants of how much psychic, magical,

and/or spiritual energy gets raised or tapped by the participants, and of how well that energy is maintained, focused, and discharged.*

Most people won't object to an emphasis on music and singing, but will balk at the suggestion that a good ceremony should also be good theater. We've been raised in a culture that believes that theatrical equals phony, and that being an actor means being a fraud. We've forgotten that what we now call theater was originally part of the ancient Greek religions (essentially, a way to lead hundreds of people in a single ceremony), and that all great performers act as mediums(!) directing energy flows between themselves, the audience, and the collective unconscious. We've also forgotten that our modern attitudes about theater have been shaped by centuries of anti-theatrical propaganda by the mainstream churches.

Of course, it's difficult for those of us who are white, middle-class intellectuals—and that's most Neopagans and New Agers, as well as most members of the liberal religious traditions —to let go and just be dramatic in ritual. We tend to be inhibited both in our scripts and our performances, and we usually fail to learn the dramatic skills we need, including the scripting, directing, and acting skills necessary to make sure that everyone feels involved at every step of the ritual (so that no performer vs. audience distinction develops). Yet if we can manage to overcome our inhibitions, our prejudices, and our laziness, our ceremonies will improve a thousand-fold in power, beauty, and glory.[82]

So let's look at some of the most important dramatic skills and tricks you will want to learn to make your liturgies as effective as possible.

Making Yourself Visible

If you are leading (or helping to lead) a ritual, it helps if everyone present can (a) see you clearly and (b) figure out that you are fulfilling a role that requires their attention. This is where theatrical costuming and prop design can give you a big hand. If your clothing and

---

* See Chapter 9 for an explanation of some of this language.

ritual tools are distinctive and easily visible in the distances and under the lighting conditions involved, then the other participants will see the cues you are giving and will pay more attention to them.[†]

Those who are in the center of a sacred space, with members of the congregation standing or sitting around them, are automatically at the focus of attention. Then you need only do something extra (move more, or less, than the others there with you) to draw the congregation's attention.[‡] The same holds for clergy standing at the front of a sacred space with the congregation behind them.

If, however, you are in among the congregation, and/or are approaching from an unexpected direction (such as the back of a temple or the outside of a sacred grove), then you must make an effort to let people know where you are coming from (so to speak) and that they should pay attention.

There are several ways to accomplish this. Raising your voice and/or speaking clearly during a silent pause will turn most people's awareness towards you. Stepping in from a circle of standing people until you are clearly separate from them will also work. Waving a noticeable object around will evoke an instinctive attention response.[§] Not surprisingly, bigger gestures with bigger props are needed for bigger visual distances.

Working effectively in a circle, which is the most common shape for Neopagan rites, requires much turning and/or pacing around, usually in a clockwise direction (at least in the northern hemisphere), so that everyone has a chance to see and hear you. Classes in "theater in the round" can be very helpful here.

Voice Control

The same advice that a drama or speech coach would give you is relevant to liturgy. Warm up your voice before a ritual begins, especially if

---

† See Chapter 6, Costumes and Props.

‡ This is called "pulling focus" and, if done out of turn, is considered very rude.

§ Especially if the object looks sharp or pointy!

you are going to be speaking loudly and/or singing. Learn to breathe deeply, from your diaphragm, and to project your voice as far as is needed. Pay attention to the different effects you can achieve by varying the pitch and volume of your voice, as well as the speed and rhythm of your words.

One theater trick to encourage people to project their voices further is for them to pretend that they are one size larger than they usually are. I suspect that this projects their aura (psychic body field) further out from their physical body, which could both relax their chest muscles for louder sound and have a subconscious psychic effect on the people viewing them to pay more attention. Another phrase used is to, "Use your Shakespeare voice!" Most of us have at least a vague familiarity with the idea of Shakespearian actors speaking loudly and clearly. Try it in rehearsals and see if anyone tells you to take it down a notch—odds? Pretty low!

Unless you are doing a ceremony that is designed to depress everyone present, *smile* while you are speaking or singing. The simple curving upward of your lips can change a funeral dirge into a song of joy or faith or triumph. We are Neopagans (or members of other liberal religions) because our beliefs are basically hopeful and positive. We should speak and sing in our liturgies as if we are glad to be there.

Safe and Effective Use of Props

Don't whack people with staves or cut them with ritual swords—it disturbs the whole ambiance. That means that you need to have practiced using these ceremonial tools under the same crowding and space conditions as the ritual will entail. Don't dance wildly with uncovered liquids or while carrying flaming objects if anyone is within spilling or igniting range (and tie your own hair up if it's at all long).

Candles, in fact, are hard to move with at all, except very slowly with big, thick-wicked candles. Candles in motion usually drip more than stationary ones, so be sure to have candle holders that will protect the hands of those carrying them. When lighting one candle from another, hold the lit candle upright and tip the unlit candle into the flame to avoid spilling wax all over yourself, your companions, the altar, or the floor. Pay attention to the flammability of *all* props that will be anywhere near fires.

Leaning staves against altars or tree trunks is usually a bad idea. They will fall over and people will trip on them. If you are going to be using staves at all, make sure that staff holders (whether objects or people) are near the place you need them to be and won't be tripping hazards themselves.

With a larger crowd liturgy, move props *slowly*. You will be further away from the other participants than you would be with a medium to small group ritual, so their ability to visually track fast motions will be less. Take as much time as is necessary to make sure that everyone sees and understands what you are doing.

The Importance of Passion

If you aren't excited about your liturgy, who will be? Yet, while strong motivation is necessary to do any effective ritual at all, actual desperation is dangerous, in that it often triggers the self-sabotaging effects of the magical Law of Perversity (also known as Murphy's Law). Mixed motivation and messages can also cause trouble, as when you are doing a justice ritual in an atmosphere of vengeance.

Boredom, on the other hand, is equally deadly. Don't assume that the mere fact that a Pagan or New Age ritual is being done will be sufficient to excite people—those days are long past. If you've been doing the same ceremony over and over again for years to the point where you can recite it in your sleep, you are likely to have a congregation full of folks who are also sleeping.

Even if tradition and orthodoxy are important to you, you can still invent ways to spice up what you are doing through music, dance, drama, costumes, or props. Spend some time meditating about what the liturgy means to you personally and what attracted you to it in the first place. Think about just how much you can change it while retaining its original (poly)theological purposes. Consider that if your rituals bore you and your congregation, then they probably bore the deities and other spirits as well, and bored spirits won't hang around much or be very helpful to you.

Remember, *It don't mean a thing if it ain't got that swing!* Try to make your liturgies at least as exciting and as interesting as you would any other activity you invest that many hours of your life into attending or leading.

When Things Go Wrong

Murphy is a great and powerful spirit. Sooner or later, something *will* go wrong. The wise liturgist plans for disaster before it occurs and thus prevents it (or at least lessens the negative effects).

The presiding clergy and the bard(s) should plan before every rite how they are going to handle mistakes and unexpected events during the ceremony, including flubbed lines, missed cues, absent people with important functions, actions going faster or slower than expected, intruders (whether citizens or officials), folks arriving late, etc.

The person who knows the script the best should be ready with lines like "Now let the ancestors be invoked!" or "Now let us thank the spirits we have had with us today!" in order to cover for missed cues. This will usually be sufficient to remind the person responsible. However, if the step is similar to ones that will immediately follow, the same sort of announcement should be made for them, so that the one first announced doesn't stand out.

If several steps of the liturgy have gone by before someone notices that a step was skipped, a decision has to be quickly and quietly made as to how dramatically, magically, or spiritually crucial the omitted actions were. If they were essential to the mana flow, then they will have to be done, though you may choose to do them quietly and unobtrusively, perhaps while someone else leads the congregation in a quiet chant or song.

Whatever you do, when a cue is missed or a step is forgotten, do *not* say loudly, "Oh my Gods! We forgot the groundhog invocation!" (or whatever it was). Nine times out of ten, none of the mortals present will notice the mistake unless you bring it to their attention. So don't.

What should you do if a prop/ritual tool is missing? That depends on how crucial it is. Most of the time you should simply adapt the ritual to do without it. Sometimes, if it's a central prop, someone can quietly leave the ritual area and fetch the missing item. Don't sneak it back into the ceremony (unless it's very small), but be either casual or dramatic upon returning. If there is no way to retrieve a central prop without seriously disrupting the liturgy, use mime to pretend it is present—and no, I'm not joking—mime can be a powerful dramatic method in ritual.

Have prearranged signals that those leading the liturgy can use to say things to each other like: "Raise/lower the volume," "Pick up/ slow down the pace," "Ooops, have everyone chant Om while I get something," "Keep them drumming until I'm ready," and so forth. These will cover a multitude of errors and omissions while you fix things, without spoiling the overall effect of the ceremony.

One of my favorites is the signal that means, "All senior officers to the bridge!"¶ If the leaders of the liturgy calmly meet in the center of the sacred space, or by the altar, or in some other prearranged spot, they can hold hands in a small circle and crucial information can be whispered through casual expressions: "I just spotted a busload of tourists pulling into the parking lot— brace yourselves!" Or, "There seems to be a small fire in the woods off to the north. We may have to stop and leave quickly. George, go investigate." Or, "We completely forgot to do the Quarter Invocations. Everyone go to their quarters and do it silently while the drummers do a heartbeat rhythm." You can always tell folks after the ceremony what you were saying, if you really need full disclosure.

As several of these examples show, the bard(s) and/or drummer(s) should be ready to sing or play music to fill in or stretch out parts

---

¶ It's best for this to be an auditory signal, since not everyone may be looking at the person giving the signal. An unscripted bell ring, horn blast, or drum roll can work well for this.

of the ceremony that are not matching the desired pacing or energy flow. They should practice such extra material on a regular basis.

Interruptions can be devastating or trivial. Fire engines and ambulances driving by your ritual space—let alone coming directly to it—can totally break the mood. A local marathon race or hostile intruders crashing into your ritual are too much to ignore, and you may have to resign yourself to disaster.

Most of the time, however, interruptions will be easier to handle. People designated to be guardians or ushers should be instructed on how to invite in people who show up after the ritual has started, how to ask parents with crying children to temporarily leave, etc.

Planes flying overhead can be ignored or, if too loud for that, simply waited out. Emergency chants or drum rhythms are again handy here when you need to pause a ceremony for a few minutes. On a few occasions when I have led ceremonies near airports, I have instructed the participants during pre-ritual briefings to chant "Aum" and hold their thoughts steady whenever a plane was overhead. This has produced very positive results in that we experienced minimal losses of power or focus.

If a physical accident happens during a liturgy, your reaction needs to be measured according to the severity involved. If a prop falls over and bangs your shin, just pick the tool up again silently. If someone trips over something and breaks a leg or catches their robe on fire, that's a sign that the deities want you to stop the ritual and take care of the situation. The *genuine* needs of the mortal participants can usually be taken as more important than the preferences of the immortal ones, for the same reasons that a child's needs are more important than an adult's preferences. The deities, the ancestors, and the nature spirits can wait for you to resume the ritual, though you'll have to reconstruct the previous mood and mana state—a difficult task with people being upset. Or you can simply start it over another day. By and large, Neopagan polytheology advocates common sense!

What do you do if some dramatic statement in your liturgy gets little or no reaction from your congregation? Take a cue from African-American church customs and repeat yourself:

Priest/ess: "So mote it be!"

Others: "Mumble, mumble."

Priest/ess: "So. Mote. It. Be."

Others: "So mote it be."

Priest/ess: "I said, 'So! Mote! It! Be!!'"

Others: "So mote it be!"

Can I have a testimony?

Let Go and Let Goddess

Sometimes a liturgy that is moving in a direction you hadn't planned isn't something going wrong at all, but instead is something going marvelously right. If we are going to interact with our deities, we need to accept that sometimes they will want us to do something other than follow a script, no matter how beautifully written or well rehearsed. Learning how to adapt to sudden divine ad-libbing or how to design and perform liturgies in which spontaneity and creativity are encouraged throughout, is a major challenge for the next generation of liturgists. In one sense, we would be moving from classical music to jazz, enabling the participants (whether mortal or not) to spark each other into a conversation of art and spirit.

This is another area where study of Voudoun and Santeria clergy techniques would be of value to us, for their priests and priestesses know how to bend to the will of a rambunctious deity without letting their entire ritual dissolve into chaos. They also know how to tell the difference between a congregant being genuinely possessed by a deity and one who is either fishing for attention or having a spiritual or mental breakdown.

Until we know all those skills, however, the best we can do is wing it. Common sense is probably a good guide here. If the goddess possessing the priest/ess says she wants everyone to jump into the river, you will have to tell her that some of those present can't swim or that the river is too polluted for safe swimming. If a fire god wants everyone to walk through the fire, you may have to tell him that your people aren't ready for that feat just yet. But if she or he just wants folks to hug each other, or sing a particular song, or play a particular game, or listen to a story, or swear an oath, then go for it!

Having a mutual conversation with the divine is precisely the point of most liturgies. If it happens in a surprising way, just accept the blessing in the way the deity wants to bestow it. Maybe you can then resume your script, or maybe you'll have to make up the rest of the ritual as you go along. Either way, you'll have an experience to remember and perhaps cherish.

Post-Ritual Cleanup and Critiques

As soon as the liturgy is over, the presiding clergy and bards should go off somewhere to remove their ceremonial gear and perform any additional grounding and centering that they might need. In the meantime, their assistants can be packing up the ritual tools and supplies, putting out the fire, etc. If there are no assistants, the presiding clergy must make sure that all fires are safely out or reliably guarded before leaving the immediate vicinity. Other volunteers should check the area to make sure nothing has been left behind, especially litter. As environmentally conscious people, we should always leave a site cleaner than it was when we arrived.

Alert Christian readers will note that on this point I agree with Catholic, rather than Protestant, clergy (as I do on many points); retiring to disvest rather than shaking hands with the congregation. Of course, with Pagan congregations, the rituals often end with everyone hugging each other before the disvestments.

Comments about the liturgy should be limited at this time to positive ones. Individuals may want to share visions with each other, or to write down any insights sparked by their experiences during it, but a critical analysis should wait until at least the next day. This is to let everyone digest what has happened and to enable any magical workings done to operate without second thoughts chasing after them on the astral.

Anywhere from a day to a week later, gather together as many of the participants as possible, to discuss the ceremony in depth. This is the time to say things like: "That new chant we wrote just didn't sound right." "George, you kept missing cues. Do we need different cues or were you having an off day?" "The harmonies on the processional were terrible. We'd better practice them some more." "Susie, your Anglo-Saxon pronunciation needs work." "The altars are too big, the dancers kept running into them." "The clergy didn't project their voices quite loud enough." "I had an insight about the wording of the consecration prayer, and I'd like to rewrite it," etc.

It's very important to state the criticisms in a friendly way, with the emphasis on creating improvements rather than assigning blame. Positive feedback about every aspect that went well should be shared before negative comments are made. People should share any psychic, magical, or spiritual events that occurred to them during or after the ritual. In effect, you should be doing the same kind of fair-but-firm critique that a theatrical troupe or symphony orchestra would have after a major performance.

Detailed notes should be kept, to be used in future planning, preparation, and performance. These notes can be copied and distributed to all the members of the group who might be interested.

Afterword

We've seen in this book that the job of a liturgical designer is to make sure that every single element of your ceremony is in a state of dynamic balance with every other part, that each stage flows smoothly into the next, and that everything your people will be doing, saying, and perceiving will contribute to the overall dramatic, magical, and religious atmosphere (while remaining focused on the target and goal).

But it's important for those of you who *aren't* creating ceremonies to realize that your liturgical designer (who will often, though not always, be your clergyperson as well) can't do it all by him/ herself. Every person participating in a ritual must be working (and playing) hard. Clergy can't do 100 percent of the psychic/magical/spiritual/ artistic work by themselves, even though this is what most people, both Neopagan and mainstream, seem to expect them to do.

I'm sure that all of the topics covered in this book have convinced many readers that creating and performing effective ceremonies requires an incredible amount of time and effort. Yes—the name of the game is *commitment*. Too many humans want the excitement and glamour of being able to call ourselves by fancy titles, without doing the *work* necessary to earn those titles. For people who did not grow up in cultures where effective magical and religious rituals are common, where everyone learns to dance as children, and where magical knowledge is commonplace, the creation, preparation, and performance of effective liturgies is a time consuming and often expensive proposition.

We have to be willing to give up quite a bit of time in order to study theater, dance, music, magic, and mythology. This isn't easy, especially if we're also trying to practice what we preach by being involved in social, political, or ecological activism. But if we aren't willing to invest the time, energy, and cold, hard cash—in other words, to make *personal* sacrifices for the deities and ideas we claim to love—then perhaps it's time we re-evaluated our motivations and personal priorities.

This kind of commitment is hard to achieve, especially for the sort of intelligent, creative anarchists who in the past have made up the majority of the Neopagan movements and other liberal religious communities. Most of us are afraid, for very good historical reasons, to have a really deep commitment to any belief system. Many of us have been burned(!) before by established religions that tried to coerce us into following the orders of mortal religious leaders instead of the Spirit(s). As American intellectuals, most of us have a strong aversion to discipline of any sort, including self-discipline. As Westerners we've been trained by television advertising to expect something for nothing and instant success, while the mainstream churches have raised us to believe that "God will do everything for you, if you just believe strongly enough." All of this cultural conditioning has been drummed into our heads from an early age and it's very difficult to overcome as adults.

Creating and performing effective liturgies, re-linking ourselves and others to the Gods and our Holy Mother Earth, actively causing personal and global transformation—this is the task of Neopagan and other liberal clergy in our time. It may be the most difficult challenge that most of us will ever face. But then, we knew this incarnation was dangerous when we took it.

After reading all these pages on liturgical design, preparation, and performance, many of you may have decided that this is all a lot of grim, dull work. Nothing is (or should be) further from the truth. Any harper will tell you that the joy of composition and performance comes *after* you have mastered the basics of your instrument and learned your scales. A painter may spend years studying color mixing, anatomy, the laws of perspective, etc., yet if there were no joy in the learning and the practice, she/he would have stopped painting early on.

Creating, preparing, and performing a ceremony requires a series of artistic decisions and actions, no matter what other polytheological, psychological, magical, or technical factors may be involved. And for Neopagans, joy is an integral part of every art we practice. Regardless of whether your liturgy is one of thankfulness or of grief, of love or of rage, of celebration or of entreaty—if it is to be a *Neopagan* liturgy, it must be filled with joy. This may be the quiet, serene joy that strengthens us in times of fear and sorrow, or the noisy, boisterous joy of friends sharing pleasure, or the wild and dangerous joy of the tigress defending her young: Balder or Bacchus or Kali. If our liturgies are truly to transform both ourselves and our world, there must be joy!

So make sure that you and the people you are working with pay attention to having *fun* during the entire process. The most elaborate modern liturgy is no more complex than putting on a three-act play, performing a symphony, or making a video documentary. Yet these are things that tens of thousands of people every year manage to do as students in *high school*— usually while having a great deal of fun at the same time.

At the front of this book, I quoted from Somé's intense work, *Ritual:* "Where ritual is absent, the young ones are restless or violent, there are no real elders, and the grown-ups are bewildered." In his book, he follows this sentence with, "The future looks dim," and indeed, for what he calls Western "machine culture," he is correct. This is why it is so important that we who understand the positive value of religious ritual, in the support of new paradigms and the preservation of old cultures, get our individual and collective acts together.

With enough determination, practice, imagination, love, and joy in our hearts, we can create ritual experiences that will have long-term positive effects on both ourselves and the entire world. And remember...

The Gods are watching us, so let's give them a good show!

Appendix

Linguistic and Historical Background

Here is some additional material about the origins and evolution of the technical vocabulary used throughout this book. *"Chambers"* refers to the *Chambers Dictionary of Etymology,* *"SOED"* means the *Shorter Oxford English Dictionary, Fifth Edition,* and *"Webster's"* is a citation from *Webster's Third New International Dictionary, Unabridged.*

Mono-, Heno-, Duo-, and Polytheism

The *SOED* tells us that *monotheism* comes from the Greek words *monos,* meaning "alone, only, single," *theos,* meaning "deity," and *-ismos,* used for forming action nouns and often referring to beliefs or doctrines— hence all the words ending in "-ism" in English and "-ismo" in Spanish.

Monotheistic deities are usually created through *hyperapotheosis,*[83] (Greek *huper,* "over, beyond, overmuch, above measure," plus *apotheoun,* "to deify"). This is the promotion of one's tribal deity to the rank of Supreme Being.

The three big monotheistic religions were created via *henotheisms* (Greek *heno*, "one," plus *theos* and *-ismos* again—*SOED*). These are religions in which there is one important deity and many lesser ones, all of whom are recognized as real deities. Those of neighboring tribes may or may not be recognized as genuine, but inferior, deities. Eventually, however, the prophets or clergy of the Top God get enough power (religious, political, economic, and military) to let them stage a divine *coup d'état*. From then on, the King of the Gods is the "Only God," or at least the only one that people are allowed to worship.

This is what prophets such as Jeremiah did in the eighth to sixth centuries B.C.E., as part of an effort to unite the warring tribes of Canaan into the nation of Israel. Before their time, they were henotheists, with each tribe considering their own ancestral deity to be the most important of the many deities they honored. Among these deities was Yahweh and his consort, whose name was variously said to be Tiamat, Astarte, or Asherah. Statues of these goddesses have been found standing on pedestals right next to Yahweh in several ancient temples (despite the supposed prohibition against graven images). The prophets loved Yahweh and hated the goddesses, so they declared that Yahweh alone was to be worshipped in the land of Israel.

Jeremiah and his followers, in consort with the political leaders of their day, then rewrote the first five books of the Torah to present an image of "true" Judaism as having always been the way they wanted it to be (much as the translators of the *King James Bible* deliberately slanted their work to please the king). The other Canaanite deities— especially Yahweh's former wives— were described as evil (though still divine), and the Jewish people were forbidden to worship them.

Most of the Jews simply ignored this rewriting of their history and went on with their personal and familial worship of multiple deities up until 100 BCE or so. To this very day, many worship the Shekinah as Yahweh's feminine side and she even makes appearances to devout Jews, like Mary/Fatima does to Catholics and Muslims.[84]

Christianity and Islam, however, took the biblical rewrites at face value. They extended the prohibition on worshipping anyone other than Yahweh with the claim that only the One God was a *real* deity and that all other religions in the world (including each other) were actually worshipping demons. Thus was monotheism brought into the world—along with inquisitions, jihads, and crusades against all who would dare disagree.

A century or so after each of these divine power grabs, however, most of the other deities slipped back into their religions under different names and titles. The common people continued worshipping their old gods and goddesses as angels and saints, pretending (at least when the religious authorities were around) that those spirits were inferior in power to the One God they were allowed to worship. Discovering that they couldn't get rid of the deities, the theologians went through various metaphysical gymnastics to explain all the lesser spirits, arguments which wound up convincing nobody but themselves.

Theocrasy comes from the Greek *theos,* plus *krasis,* "mingling," which *Webster's* tells us means "the mingling of several gods into one personality," "a mixture of the worship of different deities," and "the union of the soul with God [or Goddess?] through contemplation (among Neoplatonists, etc.)." All three of these definitions fit Wicca well.

Dualism comes from the Latin *dualis,* made from *duo,* "two," plus *–alis,* "of the kind" or "pertaining to." The first meaning presented in the *SOED* for the word is "a theory or system of thought which recognizes two independent principles." It then gives as one example, "the doctrine that there are two conflicting powers, good and evil, in the universe." This meaning was invented by Zoroaster, picked up by the Gnostic movements of 400 BCE to 400 CE, then developed by Christianity and Islam into a belief that all the spiritual forces of the universe(s) are split into good guys and bad guys.

The process of evolution is this: first a Supreme Spirit of Evil has to be invented to explain why the good God lets there be evil in the world he created. Then this spirit quickly develops into an evil God (though seldom officially *called* that). Then his minions (former deities) are said to be fighting the good God, who then needs minions of his own (more displaced deities). Celestial and infernal armies clash throughout the cosmos and various figures on both sides become popular and/or feared enough that they become full-scale deities again, despite the fact that the monotheistic theologians never call them that.

Although polytheistic faiths often have spirits of chaos and/or evil, these are seldom glorified to the heights of paranoia so common in the monotheistic religions. This is because polytheistic religions have more good spirits (and a lot of ambiguous ones) among whom to share the blame for worldly evil and trauma, and because Pagans don't usually expect their deities to be perfect. So we avoid the logical paradoxes that force the creation of an Evil God.

Polytheism comes from the Greek *polu*, "much, many," plus *theism*. Those who are not raised as polytheists often become such through *allotheism* (from the Greek *allos*, "other, different," plus *theism*), which the *SOED* rather oddly defines as "the abnormal worship of other gods." *Webster's* is a bit less biased when it defines allotheism as "the worship of foreign or unsanctioned gods." The latter definition, like that of "heresy," assumes that there is someone who has enough power to tell other people what to believe and whom to worship, a situation no longer common in the Western world, thank the Gods!

Pantheism, Panentheism, Animism, and Animatism

Pan is the neuter Greek combining root of *pas*, meaning "all." While it's also the name of the Greek God of the Wild, in word formation this isn't its primary meaning. The *SOED* defines *pantheism* as "the belief or philosophical theory that God and the universe are identical (implying a denial of the personality and transcendence of God); the identification of God with the forces of nature and natural substances" and "worship that admits or tolerates all gods."

Webster's phrases things a bit differently. Pantheism is "the doctrine that the universe conceived of as a whole is God; the doctrine that there is no God but the combined forces and laws that are manifested in the existing universe" and "the worship of gods of different creeds, cults, or peoples indifferently; also, toleration of worship of all gods (as at certain periods in the Roman Empire)."

Panentheism, (from the Greek roots *pan* plus *en*, "in," plus *theism*), means "the doctrine that God includes the world as a part though not the whole of his being," according to *Webster's*. In all these definitions both *Webster's* and the *SOED* are assuming that "God" (with a capital G) is a postulated Supreme Being.*

Animism comes from the Latin *anima*, "soul," plus the now familiar Greek *ismos*. Animism is, according to *Webster's*, "a doctrine according to which the immaterial soul is the vital principle responsible for every organic development," that is, that no living being can exist without a soul. More relevant to this book is the second definition *Webster's* gives us, that animism means the "attribution of conscious life and a discrete indwelling spirit to every material form of reality (as to such objects as plants and stones and to such natural phenomena as thunderstorms and earthquakes) often including belief in the continued existence of individual disembodied spirits capable of exercising a benignant or malignant influence."

Animatism, on the other paw, comes from the Latin *animatus*, "to quicken or enliven," plus *ism*. It means the "attribution of consciousness and personality, but not of individual spirit, to such natural phenomena as thunderstorms and earthquakes and to such objects as plants and stones."

Theology, Thealogy, and Polytheology

Most readers will be familiar with the word *theology*, which is from the Greek *theos*, plus *logos*, "word, reason, speech, account" and thus the knowledge or study of something. The *SOED* emphasizes the Christian uses of the term in its definitions: "the branch of knowledge that deals with Christian theistic religion; the original body of knowledge dealing with the nature, attributes, and governance of

---

* See Chapter 2, But What About the Supreme Being?

God; divinity," but then adds "the branch of knowledge that deals with non-Christian (especially theistic) religions," and "a particular system or theory of *esp.* Christian religion. Also, the rational analysis of a religious faith." Amusingly enough, its final definition for theology is "a system of theoretical principles; an *esp.* impractical or rigid ideology."

Webster's is again less biased, defining theology firstly as "rational interpretation of religious faith, practice, and experience; as [in] the analysis, application, and presentation of the traditional doctrines of a religion or religious group" before going on to more Christian-focused definitions.

The usual short definition of theology that most people know is "the study of God," almost always referring to a Supreme Being. This entity is usually thought of as anthropomorphic ("human shaped" both physically and psychologically), male (despite official protests to the contrary), and obsessed with real estate values in the Middle East.

Here's the definition I used in the glossary of *Real Magic,* back in 1979, and which I paraphrased in Chapter 1:

> *Theology:* Intellectual speculations concerning the nature of the God and His relations to the world in general and humans in particular; rational explanations of religious doctrines, practices and beliefs, which may or may not bear any connection to any religion as actually conceived and practiced by the majority of its members.

In 1979, feminist writer Naomi Goldenberg used the term, *thealogy,* based on the Greek *thea* for "goddess" (instead of the masculine *theo* for "god"), but she did not give much of a definition.[85] I had coined the term by 1974,[86] using it loosely to refer to "the study of Goddess"—in other words, religious philosophy with an emphasis upon the feminine aspects of Divinity.

I included this definition in the 1979 *RM* glossary:

Thealogy: Intellectual speculations concerning the nature of the Goddess and Her relations to the world in general and humans in particular; rational explanations of religious doctrines, practices and beliefs... (etc., as above).

It appears that neither Ms. Goldenberg, nor any of the feminist writers who followed her, were aware of my coinage and definition.[†] Most of them now use the word to refer to "reflections on the divine in feminine and feminist terms," as Charlotte Caron puts it. [87]

While some feminist thealogians use thealogy to refer to discussions about specific historical goddesses (usually as faces of a single theocrasic Goddess), most of them still work within a monotheistic and dualistic philosophical framework. To date there has been no widely accepted word to use for philosophical studies based upon the recognition of a multiplicity of divinities of both (all) genders.

In 1974 I also coined the terms *theoilogy* (from the Greek *theoi* for gods) and *polytheology* (based on polytheism). After many years, I've settled on the latter as the right term to use for polytheistic theology, since most English speakers will recognize the meaning quickly.[‡] For the purposes of this book, we'll consider polytheology to include every subcategory of knowledge and/or speculation that theology and thealogy could contain, but with an emphasis on the pluralistic, polytheistic approach, especially as manifested by modern Neopagans.

But who are they?

Paleo-, Meso-, and Neopaganism

The *SOED* says that Pagan comes from the Latin *paganus,* meaning "a villager, rustic, civilian, nonmilitant [that is, not a soldier or *miles*]." It goes on to define it as "a person holding religious beliefs other than those of any of the main religions of the world [apparently

---

† Or if they were, they just decided to ignore me since, after all, I do have a Y chromosome.

‡ I gave up on *theoilogy*, since it was usually mistaken for a typographical error—even when I was speaking!

Hinduism doesn't count], *spec.* a non-Christian; *derog.* a follower of a polytheistic or pantheistic religion. Also *transf.*, a person holding views not consonant with a prevailing system of belief etc. (now rare) a person considered as being of irreligious or unrestrained character or behavior."[88]

Webster's is similar, defining Pagan as "Heathen, *esp.* a follower of a polytheistic religion (as in ancient Rome)" and "one that has little or no religion and that is marked by a frank delight in and uninhibited seeking after sensual pleasure and material goods."

While there are aspects of these definitions that fit modern Pagans (we are fond of sensual pleasure and shiny objects) today those of us who proudly call ourselves Pagan use the word differently from the ways that most mainstream Westerners do. To us, as mentioned in Chapter 1, it's a general term for old and new polytheistic and/or pan(en)theistic religions and their members.

That, however, tends to be too broad a definition for many uses, so subcategories have been named, using the prefixes of "paleo-," "meso-," and "neo-" for old, middle, and new Paganism.

The Roman Church used the term *neopaganism* to criticize Renaissance artists who enjoyed depicting ancient Greek and Roman deities, while some modern historians have used to it describe the perverted Germanic Mesopaganism invented by the Nazis. The Renaissance artists may have been close in lifestyles and attitudes to modern Neopagans; however, neither artistic criticism nor Nazism has anything to do with modern Neopaganism.

Psychic and Psychical

The word psychic comes from the Greek *psukhikos*, "of the mind or soul," from *psukhe*, meaning "breath," "life," and "soul." According to the *SOED*, only the last of these, in both the mental and the spiritual senses of soul, is still used for the modern English word *psyche* and its extension *psychic*. That meaning, however, has mostly been absorbed by "psycho-," as in "psychology," "psychotherapy," etc.

As a noun, the *SOED* tells us, psychic means "a person who is regarded as particularly susceptible to supernatural or paranormal influence; a medium, a clairvoyant," as well as "the realm or sphere of psychical phenomena." As an adjective, psychic or psychical deals with such persons or phenomena. The latter version of the word is defined separately by the *SOED* as "Of, pertaining to, or concerned with phenomena or faculties which appear to transcend the laws of physics and are attributed by some to spiritual or hyperphysical agency; involving paranormal phenomena of the mind, parapsychological." The "-al" ending has become rather quaint and is rarely used today.

In Christian theology, psychic was used to mean "pertaining to the natural or animal soul, as distinct from the spirit." This usage, rooted in the ancient belief that people had more than one soul/spirit, was the sense in which the Theosophists, Spiritualists, and other occultists of the nineteenth century used it. The attitude that psychic things were inferior in virtue and value to spiritual things remains in their literature, and that of many modern groups who are descended from them.

Webster's defines psychic as "of, arising in, or relating to the psyche," and "not physical or organic; lying outside the sphere of physical science or knowledge; governed by, concerned with, or acting on the psyche or self." When referring to a person, *Webster's* says it means someone who is "sensitive to nonphysical forces and influences, marked by extraordinary or mysterious sensitivity, perception, or understanding."

Modern psychologists, by the way, still use the word psychic to refer to all sorts of mental activities, including the perception and/or manifestation of Jungian archetypes of the collective unconscious.

Magic and Magical

The word *magic* apparently comes from the *Magi*, who were the priestly caste (equivalent to the Druids and the Brahmins) of the ancient Persians, and who were renowned for their occult knowledge and skill.

According to the *SOED*, it means "the supposed art of influencing the course of events and of producing extraordinary physical phenomena, by the occult control of nature or of spirits; sorcery, witchcraft. Also, the practice of this art."

If you delete the adjective "supposed" from the definition, you'll find that most working magicians in human history would agree with most of it. The primary disagreement would be between those individuals, both practicing magicians and hostile fundamentalists (many of whom do magic themselves on a regular basis), who believe in the necessity of the intervention of spirits and those others who believe that occult (hidden) natural laws are more than sufficient to produce the desired results if used properly.

The *SOED* also mentions the figurative use of magic to mean "an inexplicable and remarkable influence producing surprising results. Also, an enchanting quality." It then goes on to mention phony or stage magic. That particular art started out as an imitation of real magic, and some of its practitioners today are still making their livings by riding on the coattails of genuine psychics and magicians.[89] This is perhaps why some modern magicians prefer to spell the word with a "k" on the end, so that real magick (so to speak) is kept distinct from stage magic. As an adjective, *magical* has no specific differences in meaning from the root word.

Here is how I define the word magic, phrased in three different ways:

(1) A general term for arts, sciences, philosophies, and technologies concerned with (a) understanding and using various altered states of consciousness within which it is possible to have access to and control over one's psychic talents, and (b) the uses and abuses of those psychic talents to change interior and/or exterior realities.

(2) A science and an art comprising a system of concepts and methods for the build-up of human emotions, altering the electrochemical balance of the metabolism, using associational techniques and devices to concentrate and focus this

emotional energy, thus modulating the energies broadcast by the human body, usually to affect other energy patterns whether animate or inanimate, but occasionally to affect the personal energy pattern.

(3) A collection of rule-of-thumb techniques designed to get one's psychic talents to do more or less what one wants, more often than not, one hopes.[90]

This last definition is often the most accurate and useful of them all, as it emphasizes the ambiguity and uncertainty principles involved.

Spirit and Spiritual

Spirit comes from the Latin *spiritus,* meaning "breathing." The *SOED* defines it as "the animating or life-giving principle in humans and animals," "the immaterial part of a corporeal being, *esp.* considered as a moral agent; the soul," "immaterial substance, as *opp.* to body or matter," and "a supernatural, immaterial, rational, or intelligent being, *usu.* regarded as imperceptible to humans but capable of becoming visible at will, as an angel, demon, fairy, etc. *usu.* with a specifying word." About a dozen or so other meanings, many of them dealing with the authenticity or real nature of a person's feelings or statements are then added. Most of the definitions for "spirit" are also given for "soul," showing the confusion between these two concepts in Western philosophy.

Webster's focuses on the negative aspects of spirits, mentioning near the beginning, "*esp.* one held to be troublesome, terrifying, or hostile to mankind" and "a supernatural being held to be able to enter into and possess a person," before going on to all the metaphorical meanings.

The word *spiritual* usually it has to do with what the *SOED* refers to as "of, pertaining to, or affecting the spirit or soul, *esp.* from a religious aspect," "standing in a relationship to another based on matters of the soul," and "of a person: devout, pious; morally good." The *SOED* goes on to mention various Christian theological opinions and the word's use as an adjective based on all the above-mentioned meanings for spirit.

Mana

Most tribal peoples make/made no clear distinction between psychic or magical energies and those we might call spiritual or psychological. Among the Indo-Europeans, for example, all of these were symbolized in the same way, by fire.[91]

The Vedic philosophers viewed this energy as having different levels of complexity and subtlety. The Theosophists brought these Hindu ideas into the Western occult mainstream as various *planes* of existence, supposedly existing at different rates of vibration, from the ordinary day-to-day world of the *Earth plane* to the most abstract *causal plane*. Despite what Western occultists have done with these concepts, it's important to remember that the ancient Hindus originally insisted upon the essential unity of these energies.

In standard anthropological jargon, mana is defined as meaning (according to the *SOED*) "an impersonal supernatural power which can be associated with people or with objects and which can be transmitted or inherited." To the Islanders, *mana* was also associated with "power, authority, and prestige."

Religion

The origins of the word *religion* are somewhat controversial. We know it comes from the Latin *religionem*, which meant "respect for what is sacred, probably with the original meaning of care (for worship and traditions)," according to *Chambers*, which also tells us:

> The derivation of the Latin was in dispute even among ancient writers: Cicero derived it from *relegere*, go through or read again … with later comparison of *relegens*, revering the Gods, pious, to *necligens*, negligent. If Cicero's derivation from *relegere* is correct, there is still little doubt that in popular etymology

there existed a strong connection with the sense of binding obligation found in *religare*, as attested among the Latin writers, such as Augustine; while Servius and Augustine derived Latin *religionem* (nominative *religio*) from *religare*, to bind fast, in the sense of an obligation on; see RELY. The spelling *religion* is first recorded about 1300.

The first two definitions in the *SOED*, for example, refer to people who belong to monastic orders, "a state of life bound by religious vows," then gives us definitions that may sound more familiar to most of us: "Belief in or sensing of some superhuman controlling power or powers, entitled to obedience, reverence, and worship, or in a system defining a code of living, *esp.* as a means to achieve spiritual or material improvement; acceptance of such a belief (*esp.* as represented by an organized Church) as a standard of spiritual and practical life; the expression of this in worship etc."

Webster's mentions modern usage first, defining religion as "the personal commitment to and serving of God or a god with worshipful devotion, conduct in accord with divine commands, *esp.* as found in accepted sacred writings or declared by authoritative teachers, a way of life recognized as incumbent on true believers, and typically the relating of oneself to an organized body of believers." It mentions monks and nuns living in "a state of religion," then goes on to add "one of the systems of faith and worship" and "the body of institutionalized expressions of sacred beliefs, observances, and social practices found within a given cultural context."

These definitions imply certain monotheistic assumptions about relations between mortals and divinities, as well as the importance of institutions in providing legitimacy, which may be why many people prefer to say they are spiritual rather than religious. If we screen out those assumptions, however, we have an accurate, if incomplete, description of religion. To complete the definition, at least from a polytheological perspective, we need to account for the magical and psychic(al) aspects of religion—precisely the aspects that most monotheistic theologians would prefer people *not* think about.

Worship

The word *worship* comes from the Old English *weorth*, "worth," and -*scipe*, a suffix used to turn nouns of rank into new nouns denoting the quality of being in that rank (as in "kingship" or "archdruidship"). Originally, the *SOED* tells us, it meant "the condition of being held in or deserving esteem, honor, or repute; renown, good reputation; worthiness, merit, credit." As a verb, it meant the "acknowledgement of worth, homage," and the "respectful recognition or honor shown to a person or thing."

Eventually, the religious connotations took precedence; as a noun, worship became "religious reverence, adoration, or homage paid to a being or power regarded or treated as supernatural or divine; the expression of this in acts, ritual, ceremony, or prayer, *esp.* of a public or formal nature."

Because the concepts involved in worship are absolutely central to this book, let's take a quick glance at what some of the subsidiary words in these last few definitions mean, again using the *SOED: Reverence* refers to "deep respect or veneration, now *esp.* on account of the object's sacred or exalted character." *Adoration* means "the act of worshipping or honoring as divine," and "(the exhibition of) profound regard or love." *Homage* meant in feudal law "formal public acknowledgement of allegiance, by which a tenant or vassal declared himself the man of the king or lord from whom he held land, and bound himself to his service; *gen.* acknowledgement of a person's superior worth, rank, beauty, etc.; dutiful reverence."

Ritual, Rite, and Ceremony

The word *ritual* comes from the Latin *ritualis*, which in turn comes from *ritus*, or "rite," which *Chambers* tells us meant a "religious observance or ceremony, custom, usage; cognate with Greek *arithmos*, number, and Old High German *rim*, row, sequence, number."

The *SOED* has several separate definitions for ritual and rite, even though most people now use the noun forms as synonyms. It's worth looking at some of each: a *rite* is "a formal procedure or act in a religious or other solemn observance," "the custom or practice of a country, people, etc.," "a religion," "a custom or practice of a formal kind, a social observance," and "a body of liturgical etc. observances characteristic of a religious denomination."

Ritual, on the other hand, as an adjective is defined as meaning "of, pertaining to, or used in a solemn rite or solemn rites," "of the nature of, or constituting a solemn rite or solemn rites; carried out as a solemn rite," neither of which is too surprising, except for the multiple uses of "solemn."§ As a noun, ritual means "a prescribed order of performing religious or other devotional services," "a book containing details of the order, forms, or ceremonies, to be observed in the celebration of religious or other solemn service," "a ritual observance or act," and "the performance of ritual acts." The *SOED* also includes a definition from the field of psychology: "a series of actions compulsively performed under certain circumstances, the non-performance of which results in tension and anxiety."

Webster's adds that a rite is a "prescribed form or manner governing the words or actions of a ceremony, *esp.* of considerable religious, courtly, social, or tribal significance," and that a ritual is (in addition to the aspects mentioned by the *SOED*), a "code or system of rites (as of a fraternal society)," and "any practice done or regularly repeated in a set precise manner so as to satisfy one's sense of fitness and often felt to have a symbolic or quasi-symbolic significance."

Two varieties of ritual are of particular interest to liturgists: *rites of intensification* and *rites of passage.* The former refers to what *Webster's* calls a "ritualistic procedure associated with periodic events or seasonal crises affecting a societal group as a whole"—in other words, ceremonies to celebrate the phases of the moon and sun, to begin or end the harvest or fishing seasons, etc. The latter, *Webster's* tells us, refers to a "ritualistic procedure associated with a nonperiodic crisis or a transitional change of status for an individual (as initiation, marriage, illness, or death)." While both of these sorts of rituals are often

---

§ Perhaps the editors of the *SOED* should have exercised the wisdom of a solemn one?

incorporated into liturgies, they deserve (and will eventually receive) future books to discuss them.

The word *ceremony* comes from the Latin *caerimonia*, meaning "sanctity, reverence, show of reverence, religious rite, ritual," according to *Chambers*. The *SOED* defines it as "an outward rite or observance, the performance of some solemn act according to a prescribed form," and "(a rite regarded as) an empty form, a mere formality."

†HAUMA†URGY

The word *thaumaturgy* comes from the Greek *thauma*, "wonder or marvel," and *-ergos*, or "working." The *SOED* defines thaumaturgy as, the "performing of miracles or wonders; magic." These days it has the additional connotation of fraud or deception, since everybody "knows" that miracles don't really happen.

That, of course, gets us into *thaumatology*, which *Webster's* tells us is the "doctrine, discussion, or study of the performing of miracles." Since other parts of this book deal with precisely how to perform miracles (at least little ones) within the context of worship services, I'll restrict myself here to a couple of fast, simple definitions of my own:

- A *miracle* is magic or some other paranormal occurrence done by or for someone who belongs to a religion of which you approve and is usually credited to divine intervention. There's also usually the implication that the act or occurrence violates (or appears to violate) "natural law," whatever that is.¶

- A *counterfeit miracle* is the exact same magic or paranormal occurrence done by or for someone who belongs to a religion of which you *don't* approve and is usually credited to demonic intervention.** This term is very popular among fundamentalist theologians, who are desperate to explain how it is that folks

---

¶ While magic, like good engineering, can *bend* the laws of Nature it cannot break them. I'm not sure that Anyone or Anything can.

** Crediting their Devil with powers equal to their God's is, of course, a heresy in Christian theology, but never mind...

who belong to "false religions" can still manage to have miracles happen for them now and then.[92]

Originally, any miracle worker was called a *thaumaturgist,* whether he or she was a holy person, a magician, or a prestidigitator (the lines weren't always clearly drawn in ancient Greece). Under the influence of orthodox Christianity, the last concept became the prevailing one.

†HEURGY

The word *theurgy* also comes from Greek, in this case, from *theos* and *-ergos,* or "divine working." Theurgy, the *SOED* says, was "a system of white magic, originally practiced by the Egyptian Neoplatonists, performed by the invocation and employment of beneficent spirits" and "the operation or intervention of a divine or supernatural agency in human affairs; the results of such action in the phenomenal world."

Webster's calls theurgy the "art or science of compelling or persuading a god or beneficent supernatural power to do or refrain from doing something; *specif.* an occult art in which the operator by means of self-purification and discipline, sacred rites, and knowledge of divine signatures in nature is held to be capable of evoking or utilizing the aid of divine and beneficent spirits" and "a human act, process, power, or state of supernatural efficacy or origin."

The idea of compelling a deity to do something may strike you as odd, especially since western ideas about deities are now purely monotheistic, and are therefore phrased in terms like "omnipotent," "omniscient," etc. *That* kind of a deity would be hard to compel into doing anything she or he didn't want to do! Yet polytheistic magical and religious systems don't always make the same clear distinctions between "persuading," "compelling," and "praying to" the Gods that modern westerners do.

A *theurgist* was a person who was using magic and ritual in an effort to contact deities or other benevolent spirits and to attain mystical knowledge. Most of the ancient Gnostics[92] ("knowers") were theurgists. They engaged in a wide variety of magical and ritual activities, including the use of unusual sex acts, mind-altering drugs, and their equivalent of rock and roll.[††]

Liturgy

Liturgy comes from the Greek words *leito,* "public," and *-ergos* again, so it originally meant "working for the public." In Latin, *liturgia* meant "public service, public worship," according to *Chambers.* The *SOED* defines it by Christian terms as "the service of the Eucharist of the Orthodox Church; a specified type or form of Eucharistic service" and "a form of public worship, *esp.* in the Christian Church; a set of formularies for the conduct of this." Among the Paleopagan Greeks it also meant "a public office or duty performed gratuitously by a rich Athenian."[‡‡]

Webster's adds that liturgy means "a system or series of ceremonial or ritualistic actions done according to a prescribed arrangement," again emphasizing some group's assumed authority.

Although liturgy is used most often in modern English to refer to the Christian (especially Eastern Orthodox) ceremony that is also known as the Eucharist or mass, it can also be defined more generally as any public—that is, extra-familial—ritual of worship, regardless of the religion involved, which is how it is used in this book.

[††] Many of these practices have been used by theurgical occultists ever since.

[‡‡] Now *that* sounds a lot like the current Neopagan approach!

BIBLIOGRAPHY

Adler, Margot. *Drawing Down the Moon: Witches, Druids, Goddess-Worshippers, and Other Pagans in America Today.* Penguin USA, 1997 (reprint).

Bonewits (Philip Emmons) Isaac. *Authentic Thaumaturgy.* Steve Jackson Games, 1998.

———. *Bonewits's Essential Guide to Druidism.* Citadel Press, 2006.

———. *The Pagan Man.* Citadel Press, 2005.

———. *Real Magic.* Red Wheel/Weiser, 1989 (third edition).

———. *Bonewits's Essential Guide to Witchcraft and Wicca.* Citadel Press, 2006.

Bonewits, Isaac, and Phaedra Bonewits. *Real Energy.* New Page Books, 2007.

Caron, Charlotte. *To Make and Make Again: Feminist Ritual Thealogy.* Crossroad, 1993.

Cox, Harvey Gallagher. *The Feast of Fools: A Theological Essay on Festivity and Fantasy.* Harvard University Press, 1969.

Driver, Tom F. *Liberating Rites: Understanding the Transformative Power of Ritual.* Westview Press, 1997.

Eliade, Mircea. *A History of Religious Ideas, Volume One: From the Stone Age to the Eleusinian Mysteries.* University of Chicago Press, 1981.

———. *The Sacred and the Profane: The Nature of Religion.* Harvest Books, 1968.

———. *Shamanism: Archaic Techniques of Ecstasy.* Princeton University Press, 1972.

Franklin, Benjamin. "Articles of Belief and Acts of Religion," in *Benjamin Franklin: Writings.* Library of America, 1987.

Goldenberg, Naomi. *The Changing of the Gods: Feminism and the End of Traditional Religions.* Beacon, 1979.

Gribbin, John R., and Stephen H. Plagemann. *The Jupiter Effect.* Random House, 1975.

———. *Beyond the Jupiter Effect.* MacDonald London, 1983.

Grof, Stanislav and Christina (eds). *Spiritual Emergency: When Personal Transformation Becomes a Crisis.* J. P. Tarcher, Inc., 1989.

Harvey, Van A. *A Handbook of Theological Terms.* Macmillan, 1966.

Haugk, Kenneth C. *Antagonists in the Church: How to Identify and Deal With Destructive Conflict.* Augsburg Fortress, 1988.

Haugk, Kenneth C., and R. Scott Perry. *Antagonists in the Church Study Guide.* Augsburg Fortress, 1988.

Heinlein, Robert A. *Stranger in a Strange Land.* Ace Books, 2003 (reprint).

Huizinga, Johan. *Homo Ludens.* Beacon, 1986.

Kushner, Harold S. *When Bad Things Happen to Good People.* Avon, 1997 (reprint).

Leland, Charles Godfrey. *Aradia: or the Gospel of the Witches of Tuscany.* Phoenix, 1990 (reprint).

Lipp, Deborah. *Elements of Ritual: Air, Fire, Water & Earth in the Wiccan Circle.* Llewellyn Publications, 2003.

Littleton, C. Scott. *The New Comparative Mythology: An Anthropological Assessment of the Theories of Georges Dumézil.* University of California Press, 1980 (3rd Edition).

Peter, Lawrence J., and Raymond Hull. *The Peter Principle.* Morrow, William & Co., 1996.

Seneca, Lucius A. *Ad Lucilium Epistulae Morales.* Loeb Classical Library #77, Harvard University Press, 1925.

Serith, Ceisiwar. *A Book of Pagan Prayer.* Red Wheel/Weiser, 1972.

Smith, Brian K. *Reflections on Resemblance, Ritual & Religion.* Motilal Banarsidass Publishing, 1998.

Somé, Malidoma Patrice. *Ritual: Power, Healing and Community,.* Swan/Raven & Co., 1993.

Starhawk. *Dreaming the Dark: Magic, Sex and Politics.* 15th Edition, Beacon Press, 1997.

———. *The Spiral Dance: A Rebirth of the Ancient Religion of the Goddess.* HarperOne, 1999.

———. *Truth or Dare: Encounters with Power, Authority, and Mystery.* Harper San Francisco, 1989 (reprint).

Story, Ronald, and Thor Heyerdahl. *Space Gods Revealed: A Close Look at the Theories of Erich Von Daniken.* Harper Collins, 1986.

Turner, Victor Witter. *From Ritual to Theatre: The Human Seriousness of Play.* Performing Arts Journal Publishing, 1982.

———. *The Ritual Process: Structure and Anti-Structure.* Aldine de Gruyter, 1995 (reprint).

Von Däniken, Erich. *Chariots of the Gods: Unsolved Mysteries of the Past.* Berkeley Publishing Group, 1999 (reprint).

Walsh, Roger. *The World of Shamanism.* Llewellyn Publications, 2007.

Dictionaries

Chambers Dictionary of Etymology. Larousse Kingfisher Chambers, 1988, 2002.

Shorter Oxford English Dictionary. Fifth Edition. Oxford University Press, 2002.

Webster's Third New International Dictionary, Unabridged. Mirriam-Webster, 1993.

Endnotes

1. Term coined by me; published in the 1979 edition of *RM*.

2. Don't confuse this word with *theocracy*, which is the rule of a society by clergy claiming to speak for their deity(ies).

3. See *BEGWW* for much more on this.

4. For some, however, duotheism is a temporary stop on the way to a henotheism in which only the Goddess will be important, to be followed by a monotheism in which the Goddess will be the only deity worshipped.

5. Term coined by me; published in the 1979 edition of *RM*.

6. Coined (I believe) by Robin Goodfellow, a Wiccan priest in Berkeley, California and published in the 1979 edition of *RM*.

7. I sometimes consider the religions that were created by the blending of Paleopagan ones with nontheistic Buddhism to be Mesopagan. Others just call them *Buddheo-Pagan*.

8. In the 1960s and 1970s the term *Neo-Paganism* (with a hyphen) was made popular in the American occult community by Tim Zell, now known as Oberon Zell-Ravenheart (see Adler, *Drawing Down the Moon*).

9. See Adler.

10. As discussed in *RM*.

11. See *RM* and *RE* for discussions of this.

12. See *RE*.

13. See *RM*.

14. See *RM*.

15. Bonewits, Phaedra Heyman; "Circle of Power" (notes from a seminar presented at the 1994 U.U. Central Midwest District Womanspirit Summer Gathering). Emphasis in the original.

16. See *RM*.

17. Seneca, *Ad Lucilium*.

18. This is known as *euhemerism*, after the Latin version of the name of the Greek writer Euemeros, who is generally credited with first publishing the idea.

19. See Von Däniken, *Chariots of the Gods*, etc., but not without Story and Heyerdahl, *Space Gods Revealed*.

20. The "disease of language" theory made famous by Max Muller a hundred years ago.

21. See *RM*.

22. See *BEGD*.

23. Kushner, *When Bad Things Happen to Good People*.

24. Franklin, *Articles of Belief and Acts of Religion*.

25. See Adler.

26. Taken from Robert Heinlein's science fiction novel *Stranger in a Strange Land*.

27. However, it's important to know that Paleopagans weren't all crunchy granola environmentalists. They hunted many species into extinction, wiped out the forests of Western Europe and the Celtic Isles, and otherwise devastated their local bioregions—all with stone axes and spears!

28. See *RM* for more on these laws.

29. For historical reasons, I have deliberately used only the male gender in this paragraph. There are female ceremonial magicians today, but the style remains a male head-trip.

30. At least within related cultures. See Littleton, *The New Compara-tive Mythology.*

31. These are the ones I have been able to research in depth. While they are ancestral to most Euro-Americans, they are not supe-rior to other cultural/linguistic complexes for any characteristic other than familiarity to most of my expected readers.

32. Eliade, *The Sacred and the Profane.* Emphasis in the original.

33. Eliade, *A History of Religious Ideas, Vol. 1.*

34. Eliade, *History.* Emphasis in the original.

35. Eliade, *History.*

36. Conversation with Deborah Lipp, author of *Elements of Ritual.* See *BEGWW* for more on this.

37. See *BEGD.*

38. I believe that the use of the Cakes and Wine ceremony, with or without a Great Rite, as a grounding mechanism rather than as one for the reception or generation of power is a mistake, for reasons I detail in *BEGWW.*

39. See *RM.*

40. Smith, *Reflections on Resemblance, Ritual & Religion.*

41. Starhawk, *The Spiral Dance, Dreaming the Dark,* and *Truth or Dare.*

42. Peter, *The Peter Principle.*

43. A *bard* was a member of the druid caste responsible for music, poetry, and other performance arts, especially as used in ritual. The modern usage of the term in Neopagan traditions can be thought of as equivalent to musical director or choir leader in many cases.

44. Harvey, *A Handbook of Theological Terms.*

45. See Kenneth J. Haugk's *Antagonists in the Church* and the *Study Guide* he wrote with R. Scott Perry.

46. Trip Gabriel, "Call of the Wildmen," *New York Times Magazine,* Oct. 14, 1990.

47. Conversation with Phaedra.

48. See *RM* for a detailed discussion of these talents.

49. See Grof, *Spiritual Emergency*.

50. This can be seen as a foreshadowing of the Reconstructing the Cosmos phase in the common worship pattern discussed in Chapter 3.

51. The burning chalice is an often-used symbol for Unitarian Universalism. It nicely reflects the common Indo-European symbolism of fire in the water or a blending of male and female symbolism.

52. Gribbin and Plagemann, *The Jupiter Effect* and *Beyond the Jupiter Effect*.

53. I am Not Guilty of inventing this one. I think Diana Paxson is.

54. The annoyance caused by many mimes, like the fear of clowns, is well worth some meditation, as both arts have extremely ancient roots in Paleopagan rituals, especially West African and Native American ones.

55. Thanks to Diana Paxson for bringing this to my attention.

56. See *BEGD* for details.

57. And then only among members of the Discordian movement (see Adler).

58. See Huizinga, *Homo Ludens* and Cox, *The Feast of Fools*.

59. Letter to the author.

60. The best place to start is Eliade, *Shamanism*, followed by Walsh, *World of Shamanism*.

61. It's interesting and ironic that Yoruba mythology— from the part of Africa where most slaves were kidnapped, and hence that of the ancestors of most African Americans—seems to be the only African myth system that exhibits the classic Indo-European patterns delineated by George Dumézil and his followers. See Littleton, *The New Comparative Mythology* and Appendix F of *BEGD*.

62. All of this ties into the magical Law of Words of Power. See *RM* and *RE*.

63. From "A Druid Worship Ceremony," published in *The Druids' Progress #2*, 1984, by the author.

64. Aidan Kelly (writing as C. Taliesan Edwards), "Why a Craft Ritual Works," *Gnostica*, March 1975. The rhyming referred to in the last sentence may not, however, be appropriate for certain cultures that did not use rhyme in their poetry.

65. Bonewits, Phaedra Heyman, "Paper on Ritual Chanting," 1992.

66. I will eventually have sheet music and mp3 files for all of these online at my web site: www.neopagan.net.

67. Driver, *Liberating Rites*.

68. I've actually heard people say this on far too many occasions. Apparently they've never bothered to consider the metaphysical and polytheological assumptions underlying this belief.

69. See *RM*.

70. Bonewits, Phaedra Heyman, "Circle of Power," 1994.

71. Although Neopagan Druid rituals may include an offering to the Outsiders, who are generalized personifications of the forces of chaos, to persuade them to go away and leave the rest of the ritual alone! See *BEGD*.

72. Propitiatory and apotropaic are standard anthropological terms; thanksgiving and supportive are my own usages.

73. Kirilian photos of plants that have been injured show sprays of energy, which many researchers think is (or is related to) mana, supposedly gushing forth out of the damaged plants.

74. See Eliade, *The Sacred and the Profane* (and numerous other titles) for much on this.

75. See *RM*.

76. Referred to in *RM* as *mantras, mandalas,* and *mudras*.

77. Aidan Kelly, writing as 'C. Taliesan Edwards', "Why a Craft Ritual Works," *Gnostica*, March 1975.

78. We took this idea from Vedic ritual tradition, wherein it is assumed that the deities take turns worshipping each other. However, it might not be appropriate for working with Egyptian or other Middle Eastern pantheons. *Do your homework!*

79. Driver, *Liberating Rites.*

80. Bonewits, Phaedra Heyman, "Circle of Power," 1994.

81. Rituals done in sacred groves are an exception, for various reasons having to do with the nature of trees and of groves. See *BEGD.*

82. For more on the performance aspects of ritual, see Driver's *Liberating Rites,* as well as most of Chapter 12.

83. Coined by me sometime before 1979, as it appears in that year's revised edition of *RM.*

84. All this theologically incorrect information has been known for many years by professional archeologists and Bible scholars. It has not, for some strange reason, been discussed much in the mass media…

85. Goldenberg, *The Changing of the Gods.*

86. In 1974 I wrote, and in 1976 published, the word *thealogian* in *The Druid Chronicles (Evolved),* a book about the Reformed Druids of North America and their offshoots.

87. Caron, *To Make and Make Again.*

88. Interestingly, we modern Pagans have finally gotten a quote into the *SOED:* "I am a practicing Pagan, I follow the old religion of Wicca"—they even capitalized it!

89. However, Paleopagan (and some Neopagan) magicians and clergy, to add drama to their work, often use sleight of hand and other forms of stage magic.

90. Taken from *RM.*

91. See *BEGD.*

92. Members of mystical (and usually dualistic) movements in the Eastern Mediterranean during the years 400 BCE to 400 CE, who strongly affected the development of Christianity and, indirectly, Islam. They can accurately be considered the first New Age movement in recorded history.